The West

Titles in the series:

The Northeast
The Southeast
The Midwest
The West
The Southwest

The West

GREENWOOD PRESS
Westport, Connecticut • London

Library of Congress Cataloging-in-Publication Data

Creative Media Applications
   How geography affects the United States/Creative Media Applications.
p. cm.
   Summary: Explores the ways in which geography has affected the lives of the people of
the United States.
   Includes bibliographical references (p.).
   Contents: v.1. Northeast — v.2. Southeast — v.3. Midwest — v.4. West — v.5. Southwest.
   ISBN 0-313-32250-3 (set) — 0-313-32251-1 (Northeast) — 0-313-32252-X (Southeast) —
0-313-32253-8 (Midwest) — 0-313-32254-6 (West) — 0-313-32255-4 (Southwest)
   1. United States — Geography — Juvenile literature. 2. Human geography — United
States — Juvenile literature. 3. United States — History, Local — Juvenile literature.
4. Regionalism — United States — Juvenile literature. [1. United States — Geography.] I.
Creative Media Applications.

E161.3.H69 2002
304.2'0973—dc21   2002075304

British Library Cataloguing in Publication Data is available.

Library of Congress Catalog Card Number: 2002075304
ISBN: 0-313-32250-3   (set)
        0-313-32251-1   (Northeast)
        0-313-32252-X   (Southeast)
        0-313-32253-8   (Midwest)
        0-313-32254-6   (West)
        0-313-32255-4   (Southwest)

First published in 2002

Greenwood Press, 88 Post Road West, Westport, CT 06881
An imprint of Greenwood Publishing Group, Inc.
www.greenwood.com

Printed in the United States of America

The paper used in this book complies with the Permanent Paper Standard issued by the
National Information Standards Organization (Z39.48–1984).

10   9   8   7   6   5   4   3   2   1

A Creative Media Applications, Inc. Production
Writer: Robin Doak
Design and Production: Fabia Wargin Design, Inc.
Editor: Matt Levine
Copyeditor: Laurie Lieb
Proofreader: Tania Bissell
AP Photo Researcher: Yvette Reyes
Consultant: Dean M. Hanink, Department of Geography,
      University of Connecticut
Maps: Ortelius Design

Photo Credits:
Cover: ©Photodisc, Inc.
AP/Wide World Photographs *pages:* 8, 13, 14, 15, 16, 20, 21, 22, 31, 32, 47, 50, 53, 54, 56, 70,
      79, 80, 83, 84, 96, 99, 113, 117, 118, 119, 120, 122, 124
©CORBIS *pages:* iii, 25, 93, 101
©Bettmann/CORBIS *pages:* 4, 7, 27, 28, 40, 42, 44, 68, 73
©Photodisc, Inc. *pages:* ix, 49, 57, 59, 74, 89, 98, 102, 105, 107, 108, 109, 110
©PEMCO-Webster & Stevens Collection, Museum of History and Industry,
      Seattle/CORBIS *page:* 66

Contents

Introduction

The West region of the United States includes eleven states. Nine of the states are part of the North American mainland: California, Colorado, Idaho, Montana, Nevada, Oregon, Utah, Washington, and Wyoming. These states are bordered by the Midwest and Southwest regions to the east, Mexico and the Southwest regions to the south, the Pacific (puh-SIFF-ik) Ocean to the west, and Canada to the north.

Two of the West's eleven states are not connected to the rest of them. One state, Hawaii (huh-WYE-ee), is a group of islands located in the central Pacific Ocean. Hawaii is more than 2,000 miles (3,200 kilometers) away from the U.S. mainland. The other state, Alaska, is separated from the United States by Canada. Alaska is bordered on three sides by water: the Pacific Ocean to the south, the Bering Sea to the west, and the Arctic Ocean to the north. Alaska is bordered on the east by British Columbia and the Yukon Territory.

The West is a region of varied landforms. The lowest point in the United States is located here, as is the highest point. The West is home to rainforests, volcanoes, tundra, deserts, canyons, seashores, and much more.

The climate of the West is as varied as its geography. Hawaii has a tropical climate. In Alaska, the winters are long and cold, and the summers are short. On the U.S. mainland, the Western climate ranges from temperate in the northernmost states to semitropical in southern California.

Mountain ranges in the region affect the amount of rainfall that different sections receive. Coastal areas, for example, receive more rainfall than do Great Basin regions. This is because the mountain ranges prevent moist air and precipitation (pruh-sip-ih-TAY-shun), which is rain or snow, from crossing them.

A Land of Rich Natural Resources

Before Europeans and Americans began settling the West, the region was inhabited by Native American tribes. These included the Paiute (PYE-yoot), Shoshone (shoh-SHOH-nee), and Ute (YOOT) in the California and mountain regions; the Nez Perce, Cayuse (KYE-yoose), Salish (SAY-lish), and Chinook in the northern coastal region; and the Arapaho (uh-RAP-uh-hoh), Cheyenne (SHYE-ann), Crow, and Cree in the Rocky Mountain area.

Up until the early 1800s, sections of the West were controlled by France, Great Britain, Spain, Russia, and the United States. Early explorers and settlers quickly realized that the region had a wealth of natural resources. Furs, fish, trees, minerals, and open land were all magnets for people looking to make a living.

Today, the West continues to be an area of population growth. From 1990 to 2000, five of the ten states that had the largest percentage increase in population were in the West. The state that grew the most was Nevada, whose population increased by 66 percent.

The Columbia River gorge divides the states of Washington and Oregon as it flows to the Pacific Ocean.

STATE BIRTHDAYS

Most of the Western states were settled after the Louisiana Purchase in 1803. The first Western state admitted to the union was California, in 1850. The last Western state to be admitted was Hawaii (huh-WYE-ee), the fiftieth state, in 1959.

State	Capital	First Permanent Settlement	Date of Statehood	Order of Statehood
Alaska	Juneau	Kodiak Island, 1784	Jan. 3, 1959	49
California	Sacramento	San Diego, 1769	Sept. 9, 1850	31
Colorado	Denver	San Luis, 1851	Aug. 1, 1876	38
Hawaii	Honolulu	*Koloa, 1835	Aug. 21, 1959	50
Idaho	Boise	Franklin, 1860	July 3, 1890	43
Montana	Helena	St. Mary's Mission, 1841	Nov. 8, 1889	41
Neveda	Carson City	Genoa, 1849	Oct. 31, 1864	36
Oregon	Salem	Astoria, 1811	Feb. 14, 1859	33
Utah	Salt Lake City	Ogden, 1845	Jan. 4, 1896	45
Washington	Olympia	Trumwater, 1845	Nov. 11, 1889	42
Wyoming	Cheyenne	Fort Laramie, 1834	July 10, 1890	44

*The town of Koloa grew around a sugar plantation started by a nonnative. Before this time, however, there were many villages founded throughout the islands by native Hawaiians. The first island to be settled may have been Hawaii.

MORE STATE STATS

The West contains some of the largest states in the nation. The biggest state in the West—and in the nation—is Alaska, with more than 570,000 square miles (1,482,000 square kilometers) of land. The smallest state in the West is Hawaii. Here, the Western states are ordered from smallest to largest.

State	Size (land and water)	Size Rank	Population	State Rank
Hawaii	6,423 square miles (16,700 sq. kilometers)	47	1,211,537	42
Washington	66,582 square miles (173,113 sq. kilometers)	20	5,894,121	15
Utah	82,168 square miles (213,637 sq. kilometers)	12	2,233,169	34
Idaho	82,751 square miles (215,153 sq. kilometers)	11	1,293,953	39
Oregon	96,003 square miles (249,608 sq. kilometers)	10	3,421,399	28
Wyoming	97,105 square miles (252,473 sq. kilometers)	9	493,782	50
Colorado	103,730 square miles (285,496 sq. kilometers)	8	4,301,261	24
Nevada	109,806 square miles (285,496 sq. kilometers)	7	1,998,257	35
Montana	145,556 square miles (378,446 sq. kilometers)	4	902,195	44
California	155,973 square miles (405,530 sq. kilometers)	3	33,871,648	1
Alaska	570,374 square miles (1,482,972 sq. kilometers)	1	626,932	8

NOTE: All metric conversions in this book are approximate.

Columbia River

1

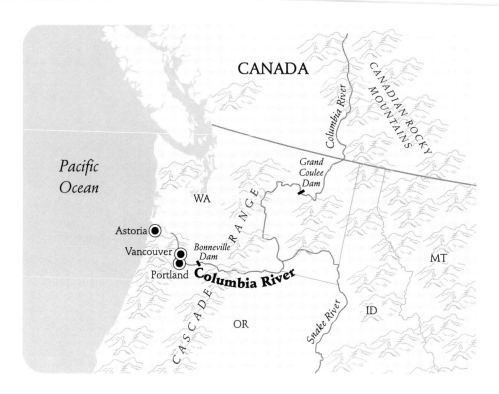

The Columbia River is the third-longest river in the United States. The Columbia stretches 1,214 miles (1,942 kilometers) from the base of the Canadian Rockies all the way to the Pacific (puh-SIFF-ik) Ocean at the border of Washington and Oregon. During its long journey to the sea, the Columbia flows south through the heart of Washington. Then the river flows west, forming the boundary between the states of Washington and Oregon for its last 300 miles (480 kilometers).

The river is one of the most important rivers in the West. During the 1800s, explorers, fur traders, and settlers used the river as a highway to the Oregon Territory. The river was the last leg of the Oregon Trail into the territory. Today, the Columbia continues to be important to the region's economy.

The Columbia is fed by many *tributaries*, or smaller rivers and streams that empty into it, including the Snake, Willamette, Deschutes (deh-SHOOTZ), Yakima, and Lewis Rivers. The Snake is the largest of these tributaries. The river is also fed by snow and glaciers from the north. In volume of water, the river is the second-largest river in the United States. Only the Mississippi discharges more water.

The river drains 259,000 square miles (673,400 square kilometers) of land—about one-fourteenth of the United States. The Columbia drains most of Idaho, Washington, and Oregon, as well as parts of Montana, Wyoming, Nevada, and Utah.

Settlement

The first people to live along the Columbia arrived about 10,000 years ago. Later, many tribes of Native Americans lived on or near the river. Area tribes included the Chinook, Clatsop, Tillamook, and Willamette peoples.

The Chinooks were one of the largest groups in the region. They used small, hand-carved canoes (kuh-NOOZ) to fish for salmon and other fish, which were plentiful in the river. Native groups also hunted for game along the river's banks. The Chinook traded with other groups in the area.

American Arrival

The first nonnative person to explore the Columbia River was Robert Gray in May 1792. Gray, a sea captain from Boston, Massachusetts (mass-uh-CHOO-setz), discovered the river's mouth during a sea-otter hunting expedition. (The mouth of a river is the place where it flows into another body of water.) Unlike earlier explorers who had spotted the river's mouth, Gray decided to explore further. He braved the wild river waters and sailed about 10 miles (16 kilometers) upstream.

Gray claimed the area around the Columbia River for the United States. He also named the river for his ship, the *Columbia Redidiva*. During the next few decades, Gray's early exploration would be the basis for American claims to ownership of the territory.

Although Gray was first in the area, the British weren't far behind. In October 1792, Captain George Vancouver (van-KOO-ver) sent William Broughton (BRAW-ten) to explore the river. Broughton spent three weeks on the river, traveling 100 miles (160 kilometers) upstream. He brought back the first detailed maps of the lower Columbia.

The first group to explore part of the Columbia from inland was the Lewis and Clark expedition in 1805. The group was sent out by President Thomas Jefferson to explore the lands acquired from France in the Louisiana Purchase. Lewis and Clark crossed the Rocky Mountains, then followed the Snake River to the Columbia.

The transfer of the Louisiana Territory from France to the United States in 1803, shown in this painting, opened the West to exploration and settlement.

While on the Columbia, the group faced waterfalls and whitewater rapids that destroyed at least one boat. At times, the party members decided to pull their canoes out of the river instead of facing its dangerous waters. They dragged their canoes downriver until they came to calmer waters.

Lewis and Clark finally reached the mouth of the Columbia—and the Pacific Ocean—on November 15, 1805. In a journal entry penned days before, Clark wrote, "Ocian [sic] in view. O! the joy!" Upon arriving, the party built Fort Clatsop on the southern side of the river. They wintered there before setting out for St. Louis in March 1806.

Five years later, Canadian David Thompson became the first explorer to travel the Columbia from its source to its mouth. In 1811, Thompson mapped the river's entire length. He would later go on to explore and map most of western Canada.

• Fast Fact •

In 1816, David Thompson was chosen to lead the team that surveyed the boundary between the United States and Canada. Thompson's survey took ten years to complete.

Struggle for Control

Both American and British explorers brought back word of the Columbia River and its wealth of natural resources. As a result, both nations were very interested in taking control of this section of North America. Not only was the Columbia River rich in furs and fish; it was important for transportation to the Pacific, as well.

During the War of 1812 (1812–1815), the British wrested control of the area from the Americans. After the war ended, however, the Treaty of Ghent required both nations to return any land to each other that had been taken during the war. In 1818, three years after the war had ended, both nations agreed to share trading and settling of the Oregon Territory.

During the 1840s, more and more American settlers poured into the Oregon Territory. By 1845, about 3,000 settlers had migrated to the region. Among the first of these settlers were Protestant missionaries. These men and women hoped to convert the native tribes of the area to Christianity.

THE WHITMANS

Marcus and Narcissa (nar-SIS-uh) Whitman were the first missionaries to settle in the Oregon Territory. The husband-and-wife team arrived at Fort Vancouver (van-KOO-ver) in 1836. They soon built a mission near what is now Walla Walla, Washington. The Whitmans spent the next eleven years teaching Native American children, as well as pioneer children. Marcus Whitman himself led hundreds of settlers into the region along the Oregon Trail. In 1847, an epidemic of measles struck the area. It hit the native people hardest. Whitman, a doctor, worked to save as many people as he could, but some natives died despite his efforts. Shortly thereafter, Whitman, his wife, and twelve other settlers were killed by Cayuse (KYE-yoose) warriors. Many others were taken hostage. The event became known as the Whitman Massacre.

The British, headquartered at Fort Vancouver on the north side of the Columbia, tried to keep the American settlers on the south side of the river. It soon became plain that this great rush of Americans to the Oregon Territory could not be stopped. In 1846, the United States and Great Britain signed a treaty allowing the United States all the land south of the 49th parallel. A *parallel* is an imaginary line around the Earth that runs in an east-west direction. Great Britain's control of what is now Canada was not affected by the treaty. The 49th parallel still stands as the border of the United States and Canada.

James K. Polk, the eleventh president of the United States, signed the treaty that set the northern boundary of the United States at the forty-ninth parallel.

"FIFTY-FOUR FORTY OR FIGHT"

Before a treaty set the 49th parallel of latitude as the border between the United States and Canada, many Americans had hoped to settle on land up to the 54th parallel, near the southern boundary of what is now Alaska. The phrase "Fifty-four Forty or Fight" became famous throughout the nation. It referred to the exact place on the map—54° 40′—where Americans wanted to draw the line between the two nations. James K. Polk used the phrase to help him win the U.S. presidential election in 1844. He told voters that he would go to war with Canada if that country didn't meet U.S. demands.

High tides and storm waves combine to form towering clouds of spray below the Cape Disappointment Lighthouse at the mouth of the Columbia River at Fort Canby State Park in Ilwaco, Washington.

THE GRAVEYARD OF THE PACIFIC

For more than a century (SEN-chur-ee), the area where the Columbia River meets the Pacific (puh-SIFF-ik) Ocean was known as the Graveyard of the Pacific. The waters there are treacherous, with high waves and shifting sandbars. Since the 1840s, more than 200 ships have sunk there, and many lives have been lost. In 1856, the first lighthouse in the region was built at the mouth of the Columbia. A few years later, another lighthouse was added to increase safety in the area. Both the Cape Disappointment Lighthouse and the North Head Lighthouse continue to guide boaters today.

Several of Oregon and Washington's first settlements were located along the Columbia River. In Washington, early towns included Longview, Kelso, and Vancouver. In Oregon, Astoria and Portland were among the first. Portland is one of the most important cities in the West. Situated where the Columbia and Willamette Rivers meet, Portland is the largest city in the state.

NAMING PORTLAND

Portland, Oregon, was named in 1845 by Francis Pettygrove, one of the city's founders. Pettygrove was given the honor of naming the new settlement after he beat his partner, Asa Lovejoy, in a coin toss. He named it after his hometown of Portland, Maine. If Lovejoy had won, the new town would have been called Boston.

Commerce

Industries that have been important along the Columbia River have depended upon the region's natural resources. Fur trading, logging, shipping, farming, and salmon fishing are just a few of the ways that people have made a living in the area.

The Fur Trade

One of the earliest industries along the Columbia River was the fur trade. The first company in the region was John Jacob Astor's Pacific Fur Company. In 1811, the company erected a trading post and named it Astoria. Astoria was the first permanent settlement in Oregon.

In 1824, the British Hudson's Bay Company set up a rival post on the opposite side of the river. Called Fort Vancouver, the site was a center of social life in the area. Many early settlers visited Fort Vancouver, the final stop on the Oregon Trail, which stretched from Missouri to the Oregon Territory.

The fur trade came to an end in the 1840s. Not only had the demand for fur in Europe dropped, but the massive trapping along the river and in other areas had wiped out much of the beaver population.

Shipping and Shipbuilding

Beginning in the 1850s, steamboats began operating on the Columbia River. The steamboats were important to trade and transportation along the river. When gold was found in Canada in the 1860s, the river became an avenue for miners hoping to strike it rich. Steamboats ferried the miners to the gold fields of British Columbia and back again. Later, steamboats carried area products, including salmon, grain, wool, and lumber.

The Oregon Steam Navigation Company was the leading steamboat operator on the river. The company had a fleet of boats that traveled from the mouth of the Columbia all the way up to Lewiston, Idaho, on the Snake River. The era of steamboats on the Columbia lasted until the early 1900s, when the railways took over.

SHANGHAIING

What happened when a boat was short of crew? In some ports, the answer to this question was "shanghaiing" (SHANG-hye-ing). Shanghaiing was another word for kidnapping. A drunken man might wake up in the morning to find that he had been taken aboard a ship in the harbor. The unlucky man was now part of a crew bound for faraway ports—possibly as far as Shanghai in China. This is where the term "shanghaiing" came from. Portland was well known among sailors as one of the worst ports for shanghaiing.

Portland started as a shipping center for the Oregon Territory. It remains the farthest point inland that can be reached by oceangoing vessels. During World War II (1939–1945), Portland became an important ship-building site. Today, it remains one of the busiest West Coast ports. Vancouver, across the river, is also an important port.

Over the years, improvements were made to the river to make it easier and safer for travel. Beginning in 1877, the Cascade Locks were built to tame a series of dangerous rapids known as the Cascades. Another set of rapids, at a place called the Dalles, was even more dangerous. Eventually, a canal was built to bypass the Dalles, too. The taming of the wild river had begun. Because of the many canals and dams on the river, barges and smaller ships can now sail far up the Columbia.

The Salmon Industry

When Lewis and Clark canoed down the Columbia in 1805, they were amazed at the amount of salmon that they saw. In his journal, William Clark wrote about thousands of salmon that the native peoples of the region caught, cut open, and dried on scaffolds. Clark and his traveling companions also relied on the plentiful supply of fish to hold off starvation during their winter on the river.

Long before Lewis and Clark's journey, early people along the river had depended upon the salmon. In the springtime, Native Americans throughout the region traveled to Celilo (suh-LYE-loh) Falls on the middle Columbia River, as well as Kettle Falls on the upper river, to cast their nets for salmon.

Each spring, thousands of salmon make the once-in-a-lifetime journey from the ocean up the river. The salmon fight their way upstream, battling the current and rapids. Upriver, the fish spawn and then die.

These yearly salmon runs were major events for the native people of the region. Thousands of salmon were taken each year during the runs. The salmon runs also gave area tribes the opportunity to meet and trade with one another.

In 1866, the first American salmon cannery was built on the river by R.D. Hume. Less than two decades later, there were forty canneries on the river. In 1899, seven canneries on the lower river created the Columbia River Packers Association. In 1901, the group expanded to Alaska, building many canneries there.

The salmon industry thrived on the Columbia River until the mid-1900s, when dams and overfishing began taking their toll on salmon populations. Dams blocked the salmon's migration paths, while overfishing depleted the number of salmon in the river. The salmon catch peaked in 1911, when 49 million pounds (22 million kilograms) were taken from the river.

Electricity

In the 1930s, the wild energy of the Columbia River was channeled for the first time to create electricity (ee-lek-TRISS-it-ee). Over the years, eleven massive dams and many smaller ones were built across the river. These dams use the energy of falling water to make electricity.

The first dam built on the Columbia River was the Rock Island Dam, constructed in 1931. Six years later, the Bonneville Dam was completed on the lower river. Built during the Great Depression, the dam employed thousands of workers who had lost their jobs during the severe economic crisis.

The next big dam was the Grand Coulee (KOOL-ee) Dam. This dam, built on the upper Columbia River, was completed in 1941. The Grand Coulee is 4,300 feet (1,290 meters) long and 550 feet (165 meters) high. Upon completion, it was one of the largest concrete structures in the world. Today, the Grand Coulee is one of the largest single sources of electricity in the world. People as far away as Chicago, Illinois (il-ih-NOY) benefit from the electricity produced by the Grand Coulee Dam. In addition, the dam's water irrigates thousands of acres of farmland.

The last dams were built on the river during the 1970s. The dams have helped the region's economy in many ways. Not only do they supply electricity and water, but they also attract other industries to the area. These industries locate near the Columbia because the dams provide an inexpensive source of electricity.

The Grand Coulee Dam on the Columbia River nears completion in this photograph taken in 1941.

Today

The Columbia River has changed greatly since Lewis and Clark traveled there in 1805. The once raging river has been tamed by the many dams that span it. Today, the river is slow-moving and tranquil. Boaters no longer have to worry about safely steering through rapids and other hazards.

Although the dams have been good for area industry, they have also hurt the yearly salmon runs. Salmon catches have become smaller over the years, even though dams have salmon steps—passageways like stairs built on the sides of dams. These steps allow salmon to continue their upstream migration. Today, most of the salmon taken from the river are born in *hatcheries*, or fish farms.

Sailboarders skim across the Columbia River near Bingen, Washington.

The Columbia continues to attract adventurers to its waters. Visitors can windsurf, fish, swim, and water-ski. In some spots, they can even try whitewater rafting and get a taste of the river as it once was.

This 1977 photo created from a 16mm film reportedly shows the legendary Big Foot in the hills of northern California.

DOES SASQUATCH LIVE HERE?

Also known as Bigfoot, Sasquatch is a large, hairy creature that is said to live in the Columbia River area. According to people who say that they've seen the beast, Sasquatch is a cross between a human and an ape. It measures a whopping 10 feet (3 meters) in height and weighs up to 500 pounds (225 kilograms). Although many have hunted for Sasquatch, it has yet to be caught. Most scientists say that there is no such thing as Bigfoot.

THE ATOMIC CITY

Richland, Washington, is known for its role in the development of nuclear weapons. During World War II (1939–1945), the first plutonium production factory was built here. *Plutonium* is a radioactive substance used to fuel nuclear reactors and weapons. Plutonium production was part of the top-secret Manhattan Project. The goal of the Manhattan Project was to create the world's first nuclear weapons. Only government workers were allowed to live in the town while the bomb was being developed. Today, Richland is still known as the Atomic City.

The Columbia Generation Station is the Northwest's only nuclear power plant. Most of the region's electric energy is provided by hydroelectric generators.

Great Basin

2

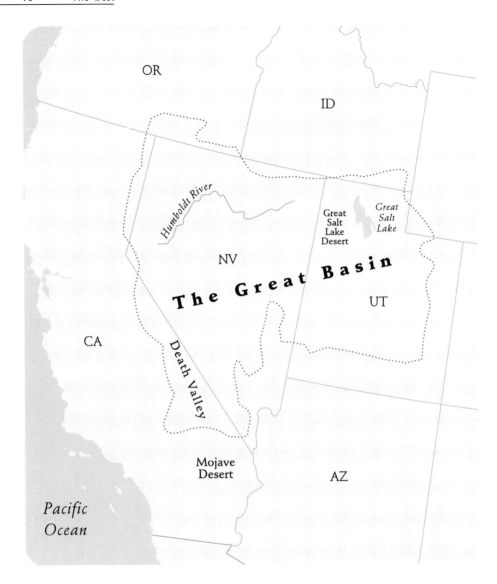

The Great Basin is a large, arid region that measures nearly 200,000 square miles (520,000 square kilometers). The area is bordered on the east by the Wasatch Range and on the west by the Sierra Nevada and Cascade Ranges. Nearly all of Nevada lies within the Great Basin, as well as parts of eastern California, western Utah, southeastern Oregon, and southern Idaho.

The area contains varying landscapes, from mountain ranges to deserts. Hundreds of mountain ranges run through the Great Basin, some with peaks up to 10,000 feet (3,000 meters) high. Deserts in the region include the Great Basin, Great Salt Lake, and Mojave (moh-HAHV-ee) Deserts. Death Valley is also part of the Great Basin.

• Fast Fact •

The Great Basin got its name from explorer John Frémont. Frémont was the first to recognize that waterways in the region do not drain into an ocean. Instead, the rivers and streams there drain into the desert.

The Humboldt River is the only freshwater stream that runs year-round in the Great Basin. However, there are many saltwater lakes found in the region. The largest and most famous is the Great Salt Lake. This shallow body of water is all that remains of a huge ancient lake that is now called Lake Bonneville in honor of an American explorer. Thousands of years ago, Lake Bonneville covered most of the Great Basin region.

Because of the vast deserts and lack of fresh water, the Great Basin region has been called "America's wasteland." The area remains one of the less-populated regions in the United States. Cities that do have large populations include Reno and Elko in Nevada and Salt Lake City in Utah.

DIFFERENT DESERTS

Not all of the deserts in the Great Basin are the same. In the south, the Mojave and the southern Great Basin Deserts are known as hot deserts. They receive very little snow or rain, or *precipitation* (pruh-sip-ih-TAY-shun). Any precipitation that occurs in hot deserts falls as rain. In the north, the northern Great Basin Desert is called a *cold desert*. Temperatures in the northern Great Basin can fall below freezing in the winter. In addition, cold deserts receive more precipitation than hot deserts, mostly as snow.

DEATH VALLEY

• *Fast Fact* •

Death Valley was given its name in 1849 by a group of gold miners trying to find a shortcut to the California gold fields. At least one member of the group died along the way.

Tourists watch a sunset from Zabriskie Point in Death Valley, California. In summer, Death Valley is often the hottest place in the United States.

• Death Valley is located in California and Nevada. Surrounded by mountains, it is 130 miles (208 kilometers) long and from 6 to 14 miles (9.6 to 22.4 kilometers) wide.

• Death Valley is the hottest spot in the United States. In 1913, the temperature rose to a record-breaking 134°F (57°C).

• Death Valley is home to the lowest point in the Western Hemisphere (HEM-iss-feer). It is 282 feet (85 meters) below sea level.

• More than 600 types of plants grow in Death Valley. In addition, hundreds of mammals, reptiles, and birds live, visit, and hunt in the valley.

MOJAVE DESERT

- The Mojave (moh-HAHV-ee) Desert is located in California, east of Los Angeles (los AN-jell-ess). It covers about 25,000 square miles (65,000 square kilometers).

- Salt flats, sand dunes, and mountains are all part of the Mojave landscape.

- The Mojave River, 90 miles (144 kilometers) in length, flows partly underground. The river has its source in the San Bernardino Mountains and ends in Death Valley.

- Borax, potash, salt, and silver are mined in the Mojave Desert.

An official of the Metropolitan Water District of Southern California points to the pipes used to pump water over desert mountain ranges from the Colorado River Aqueduct for storage underground in the Mojave Desert.

A portion of the Great Basin near Ely, Nevada, is seen from an overlook in the Bristlecone Natural Area.

Settlement

The first people to live in the Great Basin area arrived about 12,000 years ago. These early people survived by hunting for game and foraging for plants, nuts, and berries. Many of the earliest people in the region were nomadic, wandering from place to place.

Before the arrival of Europeans and Americans, several Native American tribes lived in the region. These tribes included the Shoshone (shoh-SHOH-nee), Paiute (PYE-yoot), Washo, and Gosiute (GOH-shoot). Like their early ancestors (AN-sess-terz), these Great Basin tribes were foragers. They searched for nuts, berries, and small animals. They also hunted near the freshwater springs that attracted deer, waterfowl, and other game.

In the late 1600s, life changed for the Great Basin tribes. Around 1680, many of the tribes acquired horses. Horses had been introduced into North America by Spanish explorers in the 1500s. The Great Basin tribes soon adopted a more mobile lifestyle, roaming into the Great Plains region on horseback, in search of bison. Some tribes that owned horses, such as the Shoshone and the Ute (YOOT), also began raiding some of the other basin tribes. Horses allowed the raiders to quickly attack a village, seize what they needed, and then escape.

American Exploration

Protected on both sides by towering mountain ranges, the Great Basin region was the last part of the continental United States to be explored by Europeans or Americans. One of the first Europeans to see the area may have been Francisco Garces (fran-SISS-koh GAR-sez), a Spanish priest, in 1776.

The first Americans to explore the Great Basin region were traders and fur trappers. In 1825, trader James Bridger explored the Great Salt Lake area. The following year, trapper and scout Jedediah Strong Smith made his way into the Great Basin region. Smith crossed the Mojave Desert and the Bonneville Salt Flats on his way to San Diego, California. The crossing was not an easy one. Smith and his party were forced to eat their horses in order to survive. The fearless trapper was not impressed with what he saw in the basin region. He would later describe the area as being bare and deserted.

The first American to carefully explore and map the region was John C. Frémont. With the support of the U.S. government, Frémont surveyed much of the West. With the help of guide Kit Carson, Frémont mapped the Oregon Trail and traveled through the Cascade Mountains, Sierra Nevada, and Rocky Mountains, as well as the Great Basin. His explorations and the publication of his adventures earned him the nickname "the Great Pathfinder."

GREAT SALT LAKE

• The Great Salt Lake is about 75 miles (120 kilometers) long and about 30 to 50 miles (48 to 80 kilometers) wide.

• The Great Salt Lake is up to eight times saltier than the ocean. Its saltiness is caused by a buildup of minerals through the centuries (SEN-chur-eez).

• Few species (SPEE-sheez) can live in the salty lake water. Only tiny brine shrimp and algae (AL-jee) can survive.

• The Great Salt Lake is the largest salt lake in the Western Hemisphere.

Highways to the West

As early as 1841, settlers began trekking through the Great Basin on their way to California. For those early travelers, the Great Basin was an obstacle that had to be overcome before their new lives in the West could begin. From 1846 to 1858, more than 165,000 pioneers migrated to California through the Great Basin.

Most settlers traveling through the basin followed the Humboldt Trail. The Humboldt Trail was part of the California Trail, a pathway that stretched westward from Independence (in-duh-PEN-dense), Missouri, to San Francisco (san fran-SISS-koh), California. The Humboldt Trail followed the Humboldt River 300 miles (480 kilometers) from northeastern Nevada to the Humboldt Sink, near Lovelock, Nevada. The river was too shallow for boats, so travelers followed along its banks. The journey along the Humboldt was not easy. Hostile Native Americans who lived near the river raided traveling parties. The native warriors stole horses, cattle, and other goods.

At the end of the Humboldt River, migrants faced yet another obstacle: the Forty-Mile Desert. This barren, desolate strip of desert was the most dreaded part of the journey. The bones of dead horses and oxen, abandoned wagons and goods, and the simple grave markers of those who hadn't survived the trip were common sights for people traveling across the Forty-Mile Desert.

Although the trail through the Forty-Mile Desert was rough, it was still the best way through the basin. Traveling parties that tried to find shortcuts did so at their own peril. One disastrous "shortcut" was the Hastings Cutoff. This route was popularized in an 1846 book called The Emigrants' Guide to Oregon and California. Author Lansford W. Hastings promised that his shortcut would take three weeks off the trip to California.

Unfortunately, much of Hastings's information about his cutoff was incorrect. Hastings wrote that the cutoff was shorter than it really was. He also forgot to mention that travelers would have to cross a 65-mile (104-kilometer) stretch of waterless desert, the Great Salt Lake Desert. One group who tried the Hastings Cutoff was the Donner Party. The cutoff cost

In addition to being a major general in the Union Army during the Civil War, John Charles Frémont was an explorer and surveyor, a two-time Republican candidate for the presidency (1856 and 1864), and the governor of Arizona from 1878 to 1882.

MANY NAMES, ONE RIVER

Before 1848, the Humboldt River was known by many different names—the Unknown River, Barren River, Ogden River, and Mary River. The river was given its final name by explorer John Frémont. He named the river after German explorer and naturalist Baron Alexander von Humboldt.

the group valuable time and put them in the Sierra Nevada in October 1846. The group spent the next three months trying desperately to fend off starvation and bitter weather in the mountains. Virginia (ver-JINN-yuh) Reed, one survivor, later wrote back east to a cousin. "Never take no cutoffs," she said, "and hurry along as fast as you can."

Salt Lake City

In 1846, a group seeking religious (ree-LIH-jus) freedom began a journey into the Great Basin that would change the region forever. Nearly 15,000 members of the Church of Jesus Christ of Latter-day Saints set off from Nauvoo (nah-VOO), Illinois (il-ih-NOY). Known as Mormons, the group was headed by Brigham Young and guided by explorer Jim Bridger.

In July 1847, the group arrived on the banks of the Great Salt Lake. Young liked what he saw. "This is the right place," he said, and Salt Lake City was founded. The Mormons settled in, planting crops, building homes, schools, and other buildings, and establishing a territory where they could worship freely.

Young named his new territory Deseret. It included all of Utah and Nevada, as well as parts of seven other states. In 1850, however, the United States renamed the area Utah, after the Ute tribe that had once lived there. Young was appointed its first governor. Utah eventually became the forty-fifth U.S. state in 1896.

In the following years, Mormons poured into Salt Lake City and surrounding regions. Today, Salt Lake City is the capital and largest city of Utah.

Many towns and cities in the Great Basin region can trace their roots to the Mormons and Salt Lake City. Genoa (JEN-oh-uh), the first permanent settlement in Nevada, was founded by a trader sent out by Brigham Young in 1849. Many Utah cities, including Bountiful, Ogden, and Roy, were also settled by Mormons.

This photo shows Joseph Smith, the founder of the Church of Jesus Christ of Latter-day Saints, also known as the Mormons.

THE MORMONS

In 1830, twenty-five-year-old Joseph Smith founded the Church of Jesus Christ of Latter-day Saints. Smith's religion (ree-LIH-jun), also called Mormonism, attracted followers in New York, Ohio, and Missouri.

Not everyone embraced the Mormons. Some members of the group practiced polygamy (puh-LIG-uh-mee). Polygamy is the custom of being married to more than one person at a time. In Missouri, Mormons were persecuted and driven out of the state. In 1844, Smith and his brother were killed in Illinois (il-ih-NOY) by an angry mob. Under the leadership of Brigham Young, however, the church continued to grow and thrive. In 1997, nearly 5 million Americans were Mormons. Millions of other people around the world also follow the Mormon religion.

This nineteenth-century illustration shows a Pony Express rider leaving St. Joseph, Missouri, headed west.

THE PONY EXPRESS

Between April 1860 and October 1861, the best way to get a message from east to west and back again was through the Pony Express. The Pony Express was a mail service that delivered letters and other items on horseback. Part of the Pony Express route carried riders through the heart of the Great Basin. Message carriers had to be quick and brave. During their trip, they faced rough terrain, wild weather, and hostile natives. How risky was the job? An ad for riders read: "Wanted. Young, skinny, wiry fellows, not over 18, must be expert riders, willing to risk death daily. Orphans preferred." One famous Pony Express rider was Buffalo Bill Cody, who delivered the mail when he was just fourteen years old.

Commerce

The first industry to affect the Great Basin was mining. Mining was of major importance to the region's economy from the 1860s to the 1930s. Gold, silver, copper, salt, and other valuable minerals have all been mined in the area.

The first minerals mined in the Great Basin were gold and silver. In 1859, the most famous mine in the region was discovered in Nevada's Virginia Range. The mineral-rich site would be named the Comstock Lode, after a miner who claimed that the land was his.

Although the first finds were gold deposits, the real riches in the mountain turned out to be huge deposits of silver. The Comstock Lode was the largest deposit of silver ore ever found in the United States. Once news of the mine spread, miners from around the nation flocked to the Great Basin, hoping to make their fortunes.

Between 1859 and 1890, mining boosted the region's economy—and the population. A number of towns were founded to serve the needs of the miners. One of the best known was Virginia City, Nevada. Virginia City started out as a campsite for miners. The town quickly grew with the fortunes of the miners. Soon, it was filled with mansions, saloons, stores, theaters, and hotels. At its height, Virginia City had 300,000 residents.

Other Nevada towns that were founded because of the region's rich mineral wealth included Silver City, Lovelock, Unionville, Pioche (pee-OTCH), and Eureka (yoo-REEK-uh). Because of the population boom in the area, Congress made Nevada a U.S. territory in 1861. Nevada became the thirty-sixth state in 1864.

• Fast Fact •

Author Samuel Langhorne Clemens (later famous as Mark Twain) worked as a reporter in Virginia (ver-JINN-yuh) City, Nevada. Clemens wrote for a paper called *The Territorial Enterprise.*

As mining faltered in the 1890s, so did the prosperity of Virginia City and other mining towns.

This view down C Street of the ghost town Virginia City, Nevada shows no cars or street traffic.

Borax in Death Valley

In 1872, William T. Coleman and Francis M. Smith discovered borax deposits in Death Valley. *Borax* is a compound made of the element boron, salt, and water. It can be used to make household cleaners, glass, soap, fertilizers, paint, and many other items.

Coleman and Smith founded the Pacific (puh-SIFF-ik) Coast Borax Company and began mining the borax ore. They used wagons pulled by mules to transport the borax out of Death Valley. The mules hauled the wagons 165 miles (264 kilometers) to the nearest railroad tracks. A one-way trip took up to ten days. As a result of this method of transportation, the Pacific Coast Borax Company's logo became "Twenty-Mule-Team Borax." It was named for the teams of twenty mules that hauled the ore to the railway.

Today, mining still contributes to the Great Basin economy. Mining is the second-most important industry in the state of Nevada. Copper, gold, silver, lead, and zinc are still mined today in Utah, as well.

The Coming of the Railroad

Four of the Union Pacific's most powerful figures (John Duff, Thomas Durant, Sidney Dillon, and Silas Seymour) ride in a private railroad car in this 1868 photograph.

In 1868, Central Pacific (puh-SIFF-ik) Railroad crews began working their way across the Great Basin. Their goal was to meet the Union Pacific Railroad at Promontory Summit in Utah and create the first transcontinental railroad. The railroad would connect the Pacific coast to the Atlantic coast and make travel between East and West cheaper and faster.

As the workers—many of them Chinese immigrants—moved across the West and through the Great Basin, towns sprang up to serve the crews. Although Reno, Nevada, was not started as a railroad supply town, it prospered because of the Central Pacific work crews. Later, railroad towns supplied goods and services to local ranchers and miners.

This photograph shows a campsite for a Chinese immigrant railroad crew. More than 10,000 Chinese men came to America to help build the railroad.

On May 10, 1869, Central Pacific and Union Pacific workers met at Promontory Summit, east of the Great Salt Lake, near Ogden. A special ceremony (SEHR-uh-moh-nee) was held, and a golden spike was driven in to connect the two sets of tracks together. In all, the Central Pacific built 680 miles (1,088 kilometers) of train track from Sacramento, California, to Promontory Summit. The Union Pacific had built 1,090 miles (1,744 kilometers) of track.

The train opened up travel into and through the Great Basin. More people migrated to the West. Some of them stayed in the basin region, working in the mines or on farms and ranches. For those who were just passing through, the trip from New York to San Francisco was cut from three or more months to just eight days.

The Great Basin and the Military

During the twentieth century (SEN-chur-ee), the United States military became interested in using the Great Basin for training and testing. The region's out-of-the-way location, small population, and desert conditions made it perfect for military activities. Beginning in 1951, for example, the Great Basin was the site of many nuclear weapons tests. Over the years, more than 1,000 tests were conducted here.

The Great Basin is home to a number of air force bases. Test flights of new airplanes are still conducted on some of these bases. During World War II (1939–1945), bomber pilots were trained at Wendover Air Force Base in Wendover, Utah.

One of the most mysterious military bases in the Great Basin is an air force base in Nevada known as Area 51. Located in the Great Basin Desert, Area 51 has been used by the air force to test such aircraft as the stealth bomber and U-2 spy plane. Some people believe that the base is also the site of extraterrestrial activity. They believe that an alien craft crashed near Area 51 years ago and that the remains of the space pilots may be somewhere on the base.

Today

Today, tourism has become important to the Great Basin region. Each year, thousands of people visit this unique (yoo-NEEK) part of the United States. The area is home to several national parks, including Great Basin National Park, Joshua Tree National Monument, and Death Valley National Park. Death Valley National Park is the largest national park in the continental United States.

Other attractions include such historic basin cities and towns as Salt Lake City, Elko, Reno, and Virginia

City. Visitors to the basin region can see abandoned mines, ghost towns, and salt flats. In recent years, some brave travelers have even tried to follow the old wagon trails through the basin and beyond.

Keeping the Great Basin Clean

Because of its reputation as the great wasteland of the United States, some people look at the Great Basin as a dumping ground. In 1990, the federal government decided to bury radioactive waste beneath Yucca Mountain in Nevada. However, politicians (pahl-uh-TISH-anz) and people from the area fought hard to keep this dangerous trash away.

In January 2002, the U.S. Energy Department approved the Yucca Mountain site as a final resting place for nuclear debris (duh-BREE). According to the department's plan, about 70,000 tons (63,000 metric tons) of waste would remain buried within the mountain for 10,000 years. Radioactive debris may be dumped there as early as 2010. Nevada's governor, Kenny Guinn, pledged to fight the decision.

Hawaii

3

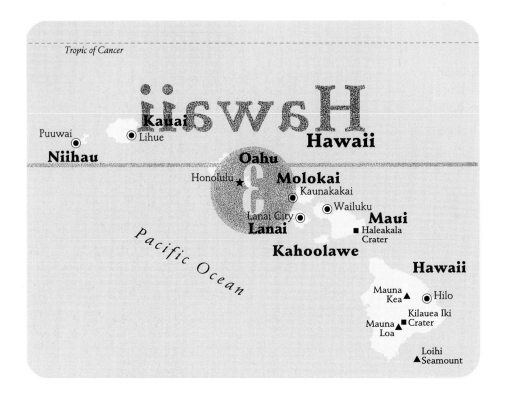

Tropic of Cancer

Puuwai

Kauai

Lihue

Niihau

Hawaii

Oahu

Honolulu

Molokai

Kaunakakai

Wailuku

Lanai City

Maui

Lanai

Haleakala
Crater

Kahoolawe

Hawaii

Pacific Ocean

Mauna
Kea

Hilo

Kilauea Iki
Crater

Mauna
Loa

Loihi
Seamount

Hawaii (huh-WYE-ee) is like no other place in the United States. The state is made up of a chain of more than 130 islands in the Pacific (puh-SIFF-ik) Ocean. The chain of islands stretches for more than 1,500 miles (2,400 kilometers), from Kure (KOO-ray) Island in the northwest to the Big Island of Hawaii in the southeast. In all, the Hawaiian (huh-WYE-an) Islands cover about 6,450 square miles (16,770 square kilometers) of land. The eight largest islands lie in the Tropic of Cancer, an area north of the equator that is known for its temperate climate. The *equator* is an imaginary line around Earth that is equally far from the North Pole and the South Pole.

• Fast Fact •

The volcanoes of Hawaii (huh-WYE-ee) are shield volcanoes. Shield volcanoes have gently sloping cones that are formed by fluid lava flows.

Located more than 2,000 miles (3,200 kilometers) southwest of San Francisco (san fran-SISS-koh), California, the Hawaiian Islands were formed by volcanic eruptions that began between 25 and 40 million years ago. Scientists (SYE-en-tists) believe that the islands were formed by a *hotspot*, a place deep below the ocean where rising *magma* has punched a hole in Earth's crust. Magma is hot, melted rock below Earth's surface. The chain of islands was formed as Earth's crust moved northwest over the hotspot.

Hawaii, the island that is the furthest southwest, is the youngest in the chain. Hawaii continues to grow today. Since 1983, 60 acres (24 hectares) of new land have been added to the island by the eruptions

THE EIGHT LARGEST ISLANDS

The largest of the Hawaiian Islands are located at the southeast end of the chain of islands. One of the islands, Kahoolawe (kah-hoh-oh-LAH-way), has no people living there.

Island	Size	Largest City	Nickname
Niihau	73 sq. miles (190 sq. kilometers)	Puuwai	the Forbidden Island
Kauai	553 sq. miles (1,438 sq. kilometers)	Lihue	the Garden Island
Oahu	608 sq. miles (1,581 sq. kilometers)	Honolulu	the Gathering Place
Molokai	261 sq. miles (679 sq. kilometers)	Kaunakakai	the Friendly Island
Lanai	140 sq. miles (364 sq. kilometers)	Lanai City	the Pineapple Island
Maui	729 sq. miles (1,895 sq. kilometers)	Wailuku	the Valley Island
Kahoolawe	45 sq. miles	uninhabited	
Hawaii	4,038 sq. miles (10,499 sq. kilometers)	Hilo	the Big Island or the Orchid Island

of the volcano Kilauea (keel-ow-WAY-uh). Another island is currently forming under the sea. Scientists expect this volcanic mountain, known as the Loihi (loh-EE-hee) Seamount, to break the surface in less than 50,000 years.

• Fast Fact •

The Hawaiian (huh-WYE-an) Islands are part of Polynesia (pahl-uh-NEEZ-ya), one of three major island groups in the central and southern Pacific (puh-SIFF-ik). Other islands in Polynesia include American Samoa, the Cook Islands, Easter Island, New Zealand, and Tonga.

Settlement

The first people to settle in Hawaii traveled there from Polynesian (pahl-uh-NEEZ-yen) islands called the Marquesas (mar-KAY-sahz). These first settlers arrived in Hawaii between A.D. 500 and 700. The Marquesans traveled 2,400 miles (3,840 kilometers) northwest in huge, double-hulled canoes (kuh-NOOZ) that resembled today's catamarans. Each canoe could hold between 50 and 100 people.

The Marquesas settlers came to stay. They brought from their homeland the seeds of trees, fruits, and vegetables, including bananas, breadfruit, coconuts, sugarcane, and sweet potatoes. The newcomers also introduced pigs, dogs, and poultry to the islands.

Around A.D. 1000, a new group of settlers arrived from Tahiti (tah-HEE-tee), an island in the South Pacific. The Tahitians quickly took control of the Hawaiian Islands. The original (oh-RIJ-ih-nal) migrants from the Marquesas may have been driven out of Hawaii, or they may have mixed in with the new arrivals.

For more than eight centuries (SEN-chur-eez), the Tahitians and their descendants (dee-SEN-dentz) controlled the Hawaiian Islands. Soon, each of the main islands had its own ruler. The kings—and queen—who would rule Hawaii until 1893 descended from the Tahitians.

European Arrival

In 1778, an estimated 300,000 people who were descended from the first Tahitian settlers lived on the Hawaiian Islands. Early that year, Captain James Cook arrived in Hawaii. Cook, an English explorer, landed on the island of Kauai (KOW-wye) on January 18. He was greeted by the native islanders as the god Lono. Legends told that the fair-skinned Lono would come to Hawaii on a "floating island."

Cook spent two weeks in Hawaii, trading iron and other trinkets with the natives for supplies. Then he set sail to the north. Cook, like other early explorers, hoped to discover a Northwest Passage across North America that connected the Pacific and Atlantic Oceans.

Cook failed in his quest to find a Northwest Passage. He headed back to Hawaii, where he arrived in January 1779. At first, the Hawaiians welcomed the explorer. Cook had once again landed in the islands during the festival of Lono, reinforcing the belief that he might be the god. However, when Cook set sail for home, only to return three weeks later with a broken mast, the chiefs became suspicious (suh-SPISH-us).

Relations between the Hawaiians and the English quickly grew worse. After some Hawaiians took a small

> **• Fast Fact •**
> Captain James Cook named the Hawaiian Islands "the Sandwich Islands" after the man who had paid for his voyage, the fourth earl of Sandwich.

boat from one of Cook's ships, the captain went ashore to demand that it be returned. The resulting argument led to a battle on the beach, and Cook was killed.

opposite:
This illustration shows Captain Cook being greeted by the native people of the Sandwich Islands, which are known today as Hawaii.

American Arrival

Soon after Cook's death, the great warrior Kamehameha (kuh-may-uh-MAY-uh) began his quest to unite the Hawaiian Islands. In 1782, Kamehameha wrested control of Hawaii from his cousin. Over the next three decades, the great chief took control of the rest of the islands. The rule of Kamehameha I ushered in a period of prosperity for Hawaii.

In 1820, the first Americans arrived in the islands—a group of fourteen missionaries from New England. The missionaries hoped to convert the Hawaiian natives to Christianity and to "civilize" (SIV-ih-lyze) them. Led by Reverend Hiram Bingham, the missionaries banned alcohol, gambling, multiple marriages, and even horse riding on Sundays. They also banned the *hula* dance, an important part of Hawaiian culture. To the Hawaiians, the hula was more than just entertainment. This sacred dance was a means of passing on Hawaiian stories and legends.

HAWAIIAN WORDS

These are some common Hawaiian words.
ae: "yes"
aloha: "hello" or "goodbye"
aole: "no"
hu hu: "angry"
komo mai: "come in"
lei: "flower necklace"
mahalo: "thank you"
mauna: "mountain"

The missionaries did make some positive changes on the islands. Most importantly, they created a written Hawaiian alphabet based on the way that the Hawaiian language sounded. The alphabet contained twelve consonants and five vowels.

In 1848, an event took place that led to American control of Hawaiian land. That year, Kamehameha III

set the Great Mahele (muh-HAY-lay) in place. This
land division allowed commoners to buy land on the
islands for the first time. Before this, only members of
the royal families were allowed to own the land.

opposite:
King Kamehameha
of Hawaii is
shown in western
clothes surrounded
by his subjects
wearing traditional
Hawaiian dress.

The Hawaiian people, however, did not under-
stand the concept of buying and owning the land.
Soon, Americans and Europeans were flocking to the
islands and buying up all of the best land. By the end
of the 1800s, foreigners (FOHR-in-erz) owned four
times as much land as the Hawaiian natives.

Hawaii's Last Monarch

From the 1840s onward, the white residents of
Hawaii began wielding more and more power there.
In 1891, fifty-one-year-old Queen Liliuokalani (lee-
lee-oo-oh-kuh-LAH-nay) took the throne after the
death of her brother, King Kalakaua (kuh-luh-kuh-
OO-uh). Liliuokalani was the first queen to rule the
islands in Hawaii's history.

Liliuokalani wanted to restore power and
strength to the Hawaiian royalty. As she tried to
take control of her country, the white business-
people became nervous and angry. In 1893, the
business leaders, directed by Sanford B. Dole,
overthrew the government and removed Liliuokalani
from her throne. Queen Liliuokalani appealed to the
United States for help. However, no help came.
Although President Grover Cleveland was not
happy that the queen was overthrown, he did not
step in to prevent it.

On July 4, 1894,
Hawaii was declared
a republic. Dole
himself took on the
role of president of
the new Republic of
Hawaii. Four years later,

• Fast Fact •
In 1993, President Bill Clinton
signed an apology
(uh-PAHL-uh-jee) to the native people of
Hawaii. The document recognized the
U.S. role in overthrowing Hawaii's
previous rulers as unlawful.

Queen Liliuokalani was the last monarch of Hawaii. She gave up her throne in 1893 when Hawaii became a republic, prior to being annexed by the United States in 1898.

the islands were annexed, or brought under U.S. control, by President William McKinley. In 1900, Hawaii became a U.S. territory, which made all Hawaiians U.S. citizens. Finally, in 1959, Hawaii became the fiftieth state.

Natural Disasters in Hawaii

Hawaii has been affected in the past by many different types of natural disasters. In the twentieth century, tsunamis (soo-NAHM-eez) and hurricanes took a terrible toll on the islands. Volcanic eruptions and earthquakes have also caused damage in some areas of Hawaii.

The natural disaster that has taken the highest human toll in Hawaii is the tsunami. A *tsunami* is a series of big sea waves caused by earthquakes beneath the ocean. These waves travel quickly across the ocean, reaching speeds of up to 500 miles (800 kilometers) per hour.

One of the worst tsunamis to hit Hawaii in recent times occurred on April 1, 1946. Early that morning, an earthquake off the coast of Alaska sent strong waves across the Pacific. Five hours later, the waves hit Hilo (HEE-low) on the Big Island. The waves destroyed 1,300 coastal homes and caused the deaths of more than 160 people.

Two years after the disaster, the Pacific Tsunami Warning Center was established. The center monitors oceanic earthquakes. When scientists at the center detect a large quake that might cause a tsunami, they send out tsunami alerts to coastal communities. These have lessened the damage done by the big sea waves.

Hurricanes that batter the islands can also cause serious damage. In 1992, Hurricane Iniki slammed into the island of Kauai. Iniki seriously damaged the sugar and tourism industries on the island. The hurricane caused the deaths of four people and more than $2 billion in damages. Other damaging hurricanes include Hurricane Nina in 1957, Hurricane Dot in 1959, and Hurricane Iwa in 1982.

Earthquakes are also an occasional threat on Hawaii. Not only do the quakes themselves cause damage, but they may cause tsunamis, as well. The last strong earthquake on Hawaii, in 1975, measured

7.2 on the Richter scale. (The Richter scale measures the *magnitude*, or strength, of an earthquake.) This big quake caused millions of dollars worth of damage.

Five of Hawaii's volcanoes are still active. These volcanoes are Loihi, Kilauea, Mauna Loa (MAW-nuh LOW-uh), Hualalai (hoo-uh-LUH-lye), and Haleakala (hah-lay-ah-kah-LAH). Scientists flock to Hawaii to study Kilauea, which has been erupting constantly since January 1983. Although Kilauea's eruptions are not explosive, they can cause property damage. Over the years, hot lava has burned down a number of homes and other buildings.

The Hawaiian Volcano Observatory, run by the United States Geological (jee-oh-LAHJ-ik-al) Survey (USGS), was founded in 1912 on Kilauea. Scientists carefully monitor changes in the volcano, including gas emissions, earthquakes, and surface uplifts. Through their studies, they hope to learn how to better forecast volcanic eruptions.

ACTIVE, DORMANT, OR EXTINCT?

According to volcano scientists (SYE-en-tists) at the University of North Dakota's Volcano World, an *active* volcano is one that has erupted in the past 10,000 years. A *dormant* volcano is one that has not erupted in the past 10,000 years but is expected to erupt again. An *extinct* volcano is one that scientists do not expect to erupt again.

MAUNA KEA

- Located on the island of Hawaii, Mauna Kea (MAW-nuh KEE-uh) is 13,796 feet (4,139 meters) above sea level.

- From top to bottom, Mauna Kea is the tallest mountain in the world. In addition to its height above sea level, it measures more than 18,000 feet (5,400 meters) below sea level.

- Believed to be dormant, Mauna Kea last erupted more than 4,000 years ago.

- In Hawaiian folklore, Mauna Kea is the home of the goddess Poliahu (poh-lee-UH-hoo).

KILAUEA

Tourists gather near the edge of Kilauea volcano to view the lava flow.

- Located on the island of Hawaii, Kilauea (keel-ow-WAY-uh) measures 4,100 feet (1,230 meters) high.

- Kilauea's crater measures 8 miles (12.8 kilometers) around, making it the largest active volcano crater in the world.

- Kilauea has been constantly erupting since January 3, 1983. This is the longest eruption in recorded Hawaiian history.

- The most recent eruption destroyed more than 180 homes and caused more than $61 million in damage.

MAUNA LOA

- Located on the island of Hawaii, Mauna Loa (MAW-nuh LOW-uh) is 13,677 feet (4,103 meters) tall.

- Still active, Mauna Loa has erupted fifteen times since 1900.

- Mauna Loa's last eruption, in 1984, lasted three weeks.

- Mauna Loa is the most massive mountain in the world. More than 10,000 cubic miles (41,600 cubic kilometers) of lava make up the volcano.

opposite:
Hawaiian legend
tells of a god who
captured the sun
and held it
captive atop
Haleakala to
give the people
more daylight.

HALEAKALA

- Located on the island of Maui (MOW-ee), Haleakala (hah-lay-ah-kah-LAH) measures more than 10,000 feet (3,000 meters) above sea level.

- Haleakala, which means "house of the sun" in Hawaiian, last erupted in 1790.

- Haleakala is still considered an active volcano. Scientists believe that it may one day erupt again.

- The first nonnatives to climb to the summit were missionaries from New England in 1828.

LOIHI SEAMOUNT

- The top of Loihi (loh-EE-hee) is more than 3,000 feet (900 meters) below the ocean's surface and still growing.

- Loihi is the youngest Hawaiian volcano.

- The seamount is located 15 miles (24 kilometers) southeast of Kilauea, off the coast of the Big Island.

- Estimates of when Loihi will reach sea level range from 1,000 to 50,000 years.

Hawaii and the U.S. Military

The battleship USS Arizona is shown sinking after Japan's surprise attack on Pearl Harbor on December 7, 1941.

The United States first recognized the importance of Hawaii's location in the late 1890s. At that time, the United States was fighting the Spanish-American War (1898) in the Philippines (FIL-ih-peenz). Because it was located in the Pacific, Hawaii was an excellent (EK-sell-ent) spot for the United States to use for its military operations.

As soon as Hawaii was annexed by the United States, the navy swung into action. The navy chose Pearl Harbor, a natural port near Hawaii's capital, Honolulu (hahn-uh-LOO-loo), on Oahu (oh-AH-hoo), as the site for its largest base in the Pacific. Workers quickly began dredging the harbor, making it deeper for the huge destroyers, carriers, and other ships that would dock there. The first U.S. warship to dock in Pearl Harbor was the USS *California* in December 1911.

Despite Pearl Harbor's importance to the U.S. military, many Americans had never heard of the remote harbor until December 7, 1941. Early that morning, Japanese airplanes flew over Pearl Harbor and bombed the Pacific Fleet. Nineteen ships were sunk or damaged. The USS *Arizona*, the largest ship in the harbor, went to the bottom of the harbor with more than 1,100 men trapped inside.

The Japanese attack killed more than 2,300 people and crippled the U.S. Pacific Fleet. The attack also brought the United States into World War II (1939–1945). On December 8, the United States declared war on Japan. Because of a treaty with Japan, Germany (JERM-an-ee) and Italy then declared war on the United States.

Throughout World War II, Hawaii served as a supply base for battles in the Pacific. The islands were also an important training site for new troops. Because of its strategic (struh-TEE-jik) location, Hawaii continued to be a target for enemy attack. The islands of Hawaii, Maui (MOW-ee), and Kauai were all shelled by enemy submarines during the war.

REMEMBERING THE FALLEN

Today, the sunken USS *Arizona* is the site of the *Arizona* Memorial and Visitor Center. Visitors start their tour at the visitor center. There, they can watch a twenty-minute documentary about Pearl Harbor. Then they take a boat out to the memorial itself. The white marble memorial is built on top of the sunken *Arizona*. It honors the men who lost their lives during the attack on December 7, 1941.

Commerce

Before the arrival of Europeans and Americans, Hawaiians supported themselves by fishing and farming. The oceans around the islands are filled with fish and other creatures. The temperate climate and mineral-rich, fertile soil is perfect for growing fruits and vegetables.

One of the first American industries on the island was the trade in sandalwood. *Sandalwood*, a type of tree found only in the tropics, is used to make furniture and other wooden items. In addition, its powerful fragrance makes excellent perfume. American merchants traded guns, alcohol, and other items for the wood, which they shipped on to China. The demand for this wood was so great that the sandalwood forests were eventually wiped out. Today, people concerned with the environment are trying to replant sandalwood trees throughout Hawaii.

In 1819, a U.S. whaling ship docked in Hawaii for the first time. Soon, the islands became a favorite stop of whalers from New England. They put into port here to repair their ships and to stock up on fresh fruit and other foods. Able-bodied Hawaiians were often recruited to serve on the crews.

Two of the most popular port towns for whalers were Lahaina (luh-HYE-nuh) on Maui and Honolulu on Oahu. These two towns quickly adapted to serve the whale hunters. Local Hawaiians knew that the whalers had money to spend, and before long, brothels and pubs sprang up. The whaling industry began to decline in the 1860s.

opposite: Workers harvest sugarcane by hand on the island of Oahu in the 1940s.

Sugar and Pineapples

In 1835, Hawaii saw the beginnings of an industry that would completely transform the islands. That year, an American planter started the first permanent

Sugarcane is processed on a Hawaiian sugar plantation in this photograph from 1953.

sugar plantation on Kauai. However, sugar didn't become truly important to the Hawaiian economy until the 1850s. During this decade, a machine was invented to separate molasses from the sugar to create white sugar crystals.

Demand for "Sandwich Island sugar" was high during the California gold rush. It skyrocketed during the Civil War (1861–1865), after Southern sugar plantations were destroyed in the United States. American interest in a constant sugar supply led to a treaty between Hawaii and the United States in 1875. The treaty allowed Hawaii to export sugar to the mainland without being taxed. In return, the United States received long-term rights to Pearl Harbor. Sugar quickly became the number-one industry in the Hawaiian Islands.

Native Hawaiians were the first people to work on the sugar plantations. As the industry grew, however, it soon became clear that more workers were needed. This marked the beginning of *contract labor* in Hawaii. Workers who performed contract labor were given free passage to Hawaii from other countries. In exchange, they agreed to work for a certain period of time. This work period might last for up to five years.

The first group of immigrants to arrive in Hawaii to work on the plantations was the Chinese. From 1852 to 1856, hundreds of Chinese migrated to Hawaii. Many chose to stay once they had worked out their contracts. The largest group, however, was the Japanese. Workers began arriving from Japan as early as 1868, but Japanese immigration soared from 1885 to 1900. In just two years, 300,000 Japanese workers arrived in Hawaii. Other immigrant groups that changed the face of Hawaii included Portuguese (POR-choog-eez), Puerto Ricans, Koreans, and Filipinos. In 2000, 45 percent of Hawaiian residents claimed an Asian background.

A second important crop on the islands is pineapples. The first pineapples were brought to the islands in the 1820s by a Spanish farmer. However, the fruit did not become important to the Hawaiian economy until the early 1900s.

In 1903, James Dole, a descendant of the earliest U.S. missionaries, began canning pineapples and shipping them to the United States. By the 1920s, the United States loved pineapples. They counted on cans of Dole pineapples to be on the shelves of their local supermarkets. To meet demand, Dole purchased the island of Lanai (luh-NYE), where he built the world's largest pineapple plantation.

Today, the sugar and pineapple industries are not as important as they once were. Although Hawaii

This nineteen-year-old surfer catches "big air" at the World Junior Surfing Championships in Maui, Hawaii.

SURF'S UP!

Did you know that surfing had its start in the Hawaiian Islands? The earliest surfers were Hawaiian nobles. These wave-sliding royals used huge surfboards that measured up to 16 feet (4.8 meters) in length and weighed as much as 160 pounds (72 kilograms).

The person who brought surfing to the United States was Duke Paoa Kahanamoku (puh-OH-uh kuh-huh-nuh-MOW-koo). Born in 1890, Kahanamoku was an Olympic gold medalist in swimming. Kahanamoku helped popularize surfing in California, and he introduced his favorite pastime to Australia, as well. Kahanamoku is remembered as "the father of modern surfing."

remains the top U.S. producer of sugar and pineapples, these items can be bought at a cheaper price from other parts of the world. Other cash crops that are grown today in Hawaii include rice, cotton, macadamia nuts, and coffee, as well as tropical flowers.

Tourism

The industry that contributes the most to Hawaii's economy today is tourism. People travel from around the world to take advantage of Hawaii's warm climate, beautiful beaches, and breathtaking scenery. Most visitors to Hawaii come from the mainland United States.

Tourism first began in Hawaii in the late 1800s. The first hotel on the islands was built in 1872. Called the Hawaiian, the hotel was built in Honolulu. An early guidebook, written in 1875, helped drum up business.

This photo shows one of the most famous Hawaiian locations, Waikiki Beach with Diamond Head volcano in the background.

Early visitors to Hawaii were usually the very wealthy—people who could afford the expensive round-trip boat ticket to and from the islands. In 1935, tourists could take one of the commercial

(kuh-MER-shul) air flights that began stopping in the islands. By 1941, Pan American, an airline company, was running daily flights from San Francisco to Honolulu.

By the 1970s, tourism had replaced agriculture as the number-one industry in Hawaii. Today, Oahu is the top tourist destination on the islands. On Oahu, tourists can stay in Honolulu, Hawaii's capital and largest city. They can visit Pearl Harbor and Diamond Head, an extinct volcano. They can also relax on one of Oahu's many beautiful beaches, including world-famous Waikiki (wye-kee-KEE).

EXTREME HAWAII

- Hawaii is home to Mount Waialeale (why-uh-lay-UH-lay), the wettest spot on Earth. Waialeale receives an average of 460 inches (1,150 centimeters) of rainfall each year.

- Hawaii is also home to Molokai (moh-leh-KYE), site of Earth's highest sea cliffs.

- Hawaii is the southernmost state in the United States.

- Hawaii is the only state found in the tropics.

- Hawaii is home to the tallest and the most massive mountains on Earth.

- The Big Island of Hawaii is the largest island in the United States.

Today

Tourism pumps billions of dollars each year into the Hawaiian economy. However, the islands' popularity has brought some problems with it. Overdevelopment, especially (es-PESH-ul-ee) in coastal areas, is one of these problems. Today, Hawaiians are trying to find ways to control overdevelopment and maintain the character of Hawaii.

Overdevelopment puts stress on Hawaii's most popular land and shore areas. In addition, an increase in people and visitors brings an increase in pollution. Tighter restrictions are being put in place to ease air and other types of pollution in Hawaii.

The skyline of Honolulu, the capital of Hawaii, stretches into the distance.

One island that has withstood the test of time and held onto its Hawaiian heritage is Niihau (NEE-how). Privately owned since 1864, the island is off limits to all but the Hawaiian families who live and work there. The island's population hovers around 250. There are no phones and no electricity (ee-lek-TRISS-it-ee). Those wishing to visit must get permission before arriving.

Pacific Ocean

4

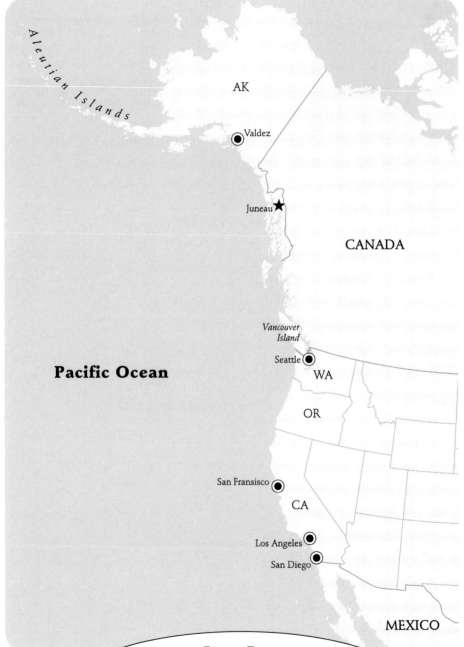

AK

Valdez

Juneau

CANADA

Vancouver
Island

Seattle
WA

OR

Pacific Ocean

San Fransisco

CA

Los Angeles
San Diego

MEXICO

Aleutian Islands

• Fast Fact •

The Pacific is the deepest of the world's
oceans. Its average depth is 14,000 feet (4,200
meters). The deepest point on Earth is located in the
Pacific: The Marianas Trench is 36,200 feet
(10,860 meters) deep.

The Pacific (puh-SIFF-ik) Ocean is one of the most important geographical (jee-oh-GRAF-ik-al) features of the West. Since the early 1800s, people from all over the United States and the world have flocked to the Pacific coast. Gold miners and other adventurers were seeking riches. Settlers and missionaries were looking for a place to call home. Today, the Pacific coast is one of the most highly populated parts of the country. Many important ports are located along the coast.

The Pacific, the largest ocean in the world, covers one-third of the world's surface. It is twice as large as the second-largest ocean, the Atlantic. In the West, the Pacific coastline (the general outline of the outer shore of Alaska and Washington, Oregon, and California) stretches more than 6,870 miles (10,922 kilometers). The tidal shoreline, which also includes the coastlines of islands, bays, inlets, and *estuaries* (places where saltwater from the ocean mixes with freshwater from streams and rivers), is more than 39,240 miles (62,784 kilometers) long.

The Pacific coast has what is called a *maritime climate*. This means that the region has a small annual range of temperature, along with wet winters and dry summers. The climate is one reason that many people choose to live on the West Coast. California's coast, for example, is one of the most highly populated regions in the nation. About nine out of ten California residents live in the coastal region.

Many islands dot the Pacific coast. Off Alaska are the Aleutian (uh-LOO-shun) Islands, a chain of about 150 islands that stretch more than 1,200 miles (1,920 kilometers) between the Pacific Ocean and the Bering Sea. More than 200 islands are situated off the coast of Washington, including the San Juan, Orcas, and Lopez Islands. California's islands include the San Miguel, Santa Cruz, Santa Barbara, and Santa Catalina Islands.

PACIFIC COAST SHORELINE

The state with the largest coastline in the Pacific (puh-SIFF-ik) is Alaska. However, more people live along the coastline of California.

State	Coastline	*Tidal Shoreline
Alaska	5,580 miles (8,928 kilometers)	31,383 miles (50,213 kilometers)
California	840 miles (1,344 kilometers)	3,427 miles (5,483 kilometers)
Oregon	296 miles (474 kilometers)	1,410 miles (2,256 kilometers)
Washington	157 miles (251 kilometers)	3,026 miles (4,842 kilometers)

* Tidal shoreline includes the shoreline of islands, bays, inlets, and estuaries (places where saltwater from the ocean mixes with freshwater from streams and rivers).

Exploration and Settlement

The first people to settle in North America migrated here thousands of years ago from Asia. These early people crossed from continent to continent on a large corridor of land now called the Bering Land Bridge. The Bering Land Bridge stretched across the Bering Sea between what is now Russia and Alaska. As the climate warmed and glaciers melted, sea levels rose, covering the bridge between the continents.

• Fast Fact •

The Bering Land Bridge National Preserve is located near Nome, Alaska. The preserve contains 2.7 million acres (1.08 million hectares) of wilderness.

Those who crossed the Bering Land Bridge gradually migrated throughout the continent, becoming the first settlers in North America. Some of the first groups along the Pacific coast settled there more than 12,000 years ago.

Later tribal groups along the coast were descended from these first travelers. Before the arrival of Europeans in the early 1500s, there were hundreds of thousands of native peoples living along the Pacific coast. Coastal tribes included the Aleut, Tlingit (TLIN-git), and Haida (HYE-duh) in Alaska; the Nootka (NOOT-kuh) and Coast Salish (SAY-lish) in Washington; the Chinook in Washington and Oregon; and the Hupa, Yurok, and Pomo in California.

Coastal tribes took advantage of the wealth of natural resources around them. They fished in the ocean and nearby rivers. They hunted deer in the forests and seals and sea lions on the coast. They also used wood from forest trees to make homes and tools.

Some of the coastal tribes carved huge, oceangoing canoes (kuh-NOOZ). The Nootka and Tlingit used the canoes to catch fish and whales in the Pacific. Some California tribes built boats to hunt sea lions, dolphins, and other creatures.

PACIFIC COAST STATES

- The name *Alaska* may come from the native Aleut word *alakshak*, meaning "the mainland" or "great land."

- The only state named for a president, Washington was named after first president George Washington in 1853.

- No one is certain of the origin (OR-ih-jin) of the name *Oregon*. Some think that the name may come from the French word *ouragan*, meaning "storm."

- Named by explorer Juan Rodríguez Cabrillo (kah-BREE-oh) in 1542, California probably got its name from a 1510 Spanish novel in which an island paradise is called Califia.

These Sitka men wear ceremonial robes as they perform a dance during a potlatch in Klukwan, Alaska.

POTLATCH!

Some tribes of the northern Pacific coast really knew how to party. Such groups as the Chinook and Kwakiutl (kwah-kee-YOOT-ul) held *potlatches*, huge parties during which the host gave away gifts to the guests. A potlatch might be held to celebrate (SEL-uh-brayt) an important family occasion, including a death or a marriage. Before the gift giving, partygoers were treated to dinner, dancing, and speeches. Potlatches were used by tribal families to show others how wealthy they were. The richer the family, the bigger and more elaborate the potlatch.

Some Pacific coast groups also made tall, colorful pieces of art called *totem* poles. These carved wooden posts came in all sizes, from 10 feet (3 meters) up to 70 feet (21 meters) in height. Animal figures, including eagles, bears, whales, and frogs, decorated each pole. The animals often represented people, families, or tribes. On some poles, the carvings told a story. Other poles were carved after a tribal member died, as a sort of memorial to the person.

European Arrival

The first Europeans to explore the Pacific coast area were the Spanish. Two of the earliest Spanish explorers along the coast were Juan Rodríguez Cabrillo (kah-BREE-oh) and Bartolomé Ferrelo (fuh-RAY-oh). In September 1542, Cabrillo sailed into San Diego Bay. He continued up the California coast, claiming the entire area for Spain. The same year, Ferrelo may have sailed as far up the coast as southern Oregon. However, Ferrelo and his crew did not bother to land and explore the coastal area.

The second explorer to venture ashore was England's Sir Francis Drake. In 1577, Drake was sent to the Pacific coast of the New World by Queen Elizabeth I. His mission was to attack Spanish settlements there.

After plundering several Spanish ports along the coast, Drake sailed north. He was looking for a shortcut across North America, a water route back to the Atlantic. This much sought-after route—which did not exist—was called the Northwest Passage.

• **Fast Fact** •

Sir Francis Drake was the first Englishman to sail around the world.

This engraving shows Sir Francis Drake, the English sailor who explored the coast of what today is known as California.

In 1579, Drake landed just north of what is now San Francisco (san fran-SISS-koh), California. He claimed the area for England, naming it New Albion (AL-bee-en). Drake may have continued as far north as Oregon, but he eventually turned back.

Spanish Missions

Despite Drake's adventure, the Spanish continued to be the strongest force along the southern coast. The first permanent settlements along the Pacific coast were missions, founded by Franciscan (fran-SISS-kan) priests. The Franciscans hoped to convert the native tribes to Christianity. They also hoped to make the native peoples loyal Spanish subjects.

To help with their conversion, priests often brought the natives to live at the mission settlements. They were given European-style clothing, taught Spanish, and encouraged to give up their native traditions. They also worked at the mission as laborers, building the missions and *presidios*, or forts, that the Spanish constructed throughout the area.

The first of the Spanish missions—and the first permanent settlement in California—was built in San Diego in 1769. Called San Diego de Alcalá (ahl-kah-LAH), the mission was the southernmost of a string of twenty-one missions stretching northward up the California coast. The northernmost mission, located in Sonoma, was built in 1823.

The age of the missions ended in the 1830s, when the last of the settlements was taken out of the hands of the Franciscans. Many of the mission lands were given away, mostly to Spanish people who settled in California.

• *Fast Fact* •
The string of twenty-one Franciscan (fran-SISS-kan) missions built in California were connected by a road called *El Camino Reál*, or "the Royal Road." The road was named in honor of Spain's king.

SAN JUAN CAPISTRANO

San Juan Capistrano, founded in 1776, was the seventh of the twenty-one coastal missions built in California. Over the years, it has become famous for an amazing spring event. Every year, around March 19, hundreds of swallows return to San Juan Capistrano from Goya, Argentina (ar-jen-TEE-nah). The birds travel more than 7,000 miles (11,200 kilometers) during their thirty-day return trip to California. Mission bells are rung when the first swallow comes into view, and a festival is held to celebrate (SEL-uh-brayt).

The Russians in Alaska

While the Spanish were busy along the southern coast of the Pacific, the Russians were dominating the northern coastline. One of the earliest Russian expeditions to what is now Alaska was led by Vitus Bering in 1741. Bering, a Danish navigator working for Russia, landed at what is now Prince William Sound in Alaska.

On the trip home, disaster struck Bering and his crew. First, many of the men came down with *scurvy*. Scurvy is a disease caused by a lack of vitamin C. It was a common condition for sailors, who went months at sea without eating fresh fruits or vegetables. To make matters worse, Bering was shipwrecked on the Aleutian Islands. The explorer and half his crew died there.

Gold seekers such as these, shown in this 1897 photograph, risked their lives to cross Chilkoot Pass to reach Alaskan gold fields.

However, the rest of the men were able to build a boat and sail back to Russia. They brought with them news of a land filled with seals and sea otters, animals prized for their skins. Before long, Russian fur hunters and traders made their way to the

Aleutians. The Russians forced native Aleuts to hunt and trap for them.

As the Russians realized the wealth of natural resources in the New World, they began moving south, exploring and hunting along the Pacific coast. In 1812, a Russian fur company founded a trading post about 100 miles (160 kilometers) north of San Francisco called Fort Ross. Although Fort Ross did not prove to be as profitable as the Russians had hoped, it played an important role in California history. In 1841, the Russian company sold the outpost to German settler John Sutter. Seven years later, gold found at Sutter's Mill set off the California gold rush.

ALASKA, THE FORTY-NINTH STATE

In spring of 1867, the United States purchased Alaska from Russia. U.S. secretary of state William H. Seward arranged the sale, which cost the American government $7.2 million—just 1.9 cents per acre of land. Despite Seward's shrewd bargaining, many felt that the purchase was not a good one. Alaska became known as "Seward's icebox" and "Seward's folly."

Contested Land

The English also staked a claim along the Pacific coast. In 1778, Captain James Cook charted the Washington coast, as well as Vancouver (van-KOO-ver) Island. Cook claimed the region for England. Then he set sail for home, taking with him a shipment of goods that would spark new settlement in the area: furs. In 1785, British fur traders began heading to the Pacific coast.

The Spanish, of course, were not happy about the British coming into what the Spanish considered their territory. After much tension and a few serious international incidents (IN-sih-dents), however, the two nations hammered out the Nootka Sound Convention. By signing the 1790 treaty, Spain gave complete control of the northern Pacific coast to Great Britain.

Yet even as Britain gained control of the area from Spain, another nation began asserting its claim to the area. In 1788, American captain Robert Gray had sailed to the Oregon coast to trade furs. In 1792, Gray returned for a second trip. This time, Gray explored the Columbia River, claiming the area for the United States. Soon, Great Britain would square off with the United States for control of the northern Pacific coast. Not until 1846 would the two nations agree upon the division between U.S. and British territory.

LEWIS AND CLARK REACH THE PACIFIC

In December 1805, Meriwether Lewis and William Clark finally attained the goal of their expedition: to reach the Pacific Ocean. Over the past eighteen months, the group had traveled over the Great Plains, across the Rocky Mountains, and down the Columbia River before reaching the Pacific. The explorers constructed Fort Clatsop, near what is now Astoria, and settled in for the winter. They remained on the coast until March 1806. The Lewis and Clark expedition put an end to the idea that a Northwest Passage across North America might exist.

Americans on the West Coast

In September 1806, explorers Meriwether Lewis and William Clark returned from their historic trek to the Pacific coast. They brought back tales of the land beyond the Rockies. Their accounts of adventure and natural riches sparked a great deal of American interest in the lands out west. In the 1840s, the first wagon trains to the West began.

The earliest American homesteaders traveled to California and other Pacific coast regions along the Santa Fe Trail, the Oregon Trail, and the California Trail. The trip was not easy. Settlers crossed plains, mountains, and deserts. They sometimes faced hostile native people who wanted them off the native lands.

Upon arriving on the coast, settlers found an agreeable climate and plenty of ways to earn a good living. However, the area had been under the control of Mexico since 1821, when that nation had declared its independence (in-duh-PEN-dense) from Spain. American settlers did not want to obey Mexican rule. On June 14, 1846, the Bear Flag Revolt took place. American settlers in California captured a Mexican fort north of San Francisco. Then they declared American settlements along the coast to be parts of an independent republic.

The new nation didn't last long. Less than one month later, the U.S. Navy sailed into Monterey Bay and claimed California as part of the United States. However, Mexico was not about to give the area up without a fight. The battle for control of California was one of the causes of the Mexican War (1846–1848).

The Mexican War ended on February 2, 1848, when the two battling nations signed the Treaty of Guadalupe Hidalgo (gwahd-uh-LOOP hih-DAHL-goh). Under the terms of the treaty, Mexico gave all of California, Texas, and other southwestern land to the United States for a sum of $15 million.

This painting depicts the Battle of Palo Alto, the first battle of the Mexican War in 1846.

The Golden Gate Bridge, completed in 1937, was built during the Great Depression for a cost of $35 million.

THE GOLDEN GATE
AND ITS FAMOUS BRIDGE

Many people have heard of the Golden Gate Bridge. Did you know that the Golden Gate is actually the 5-mile (8-kilometer) long strait of water that connects the Pacific Ocean to San Francisco (san fran-SISS-koh) Bay? The strait was named by American explorer John Charles Frémont in 1846.

> • Fast Fact •
> The Golden Gate Bridge is more than 9,200 feet
> (2,760 meters) long and 746 feet (224 meters) high.
> One of the longest suspension bridges in the world,
> the Golden Gate Bridge connects San Francisco to
> Marin County.

Natural Disasters

A unique (yoo-NEEK) geographic (jee-oh-GRAF-ik) feature of the Pacific coast has affected those who live there since the earliest days of settlement. Two plates of Earth's crust meet near the coastline. When the plates rub together, the result is an earthquake.

One of the most famous earthquake areas in the world is along the San Andreas Fault. The San Andreas Fault is a series of fractures in the Earth's crust. The fractures parallel the Pacific coast, stretching more than 600 miles (960 kilometers) across much of California. The area is a hotspot for earthquake activity.

Another type of natural disaster that can pose a threat along the coast is a tsunami (soo-NAHM-ee). A *tsunami* is a series of waves set off by an earthquake deep in the ocean. Tsunamis travel quickly across the sea, sometimes moving at speeds of up to 500 miles (800 kilometers) per hour. Tsunamis can cause serious damage thousands of miles from their points of origin (OR-ih-jin).

One memorable earthquake and its resulting tsunami struck the Pacific coast on March 27, 1964. Known as the Good Friday earthquake, the tremor measured between 8.4 and 8.6 on the Richter scale.

> • Fast Fact •
> The Richter scale measures the magnitude, or
> strength, of an earthquake. Any earthquake that
> measures above 7.0 is considered a major quake.

For four long minutes, the earth along the Pacific coast of Alaska rattled and shook. This powerful earthquake and the resulting tsunami killed 130 people and caused more than $200 million in damage. The Alaskan port towns of Valdez and Chenega were severely damaged.

BIG QUAKES ALONG THE SAN ANDREAS FAULT

December 8, 1812: A huge earthquake damages or destroys many of California's coastal missions. San Juan Capistrano is especially (es-PESH-ul-ee) hard hit. Although the quake occurs before the invention of the Richter scale, scientists believe that it may have been as strong as 7.5.

January 9, 1857: A quake occurs near Fort Tejon (tay-HOHN), an army post near Lebec, California. Geologists (jee-AHL-oh-jists) estimate it as one of the strongest ever felt in the United States. Only two people are killed because the quake is in an area with few residents.

April 18, 1906: An earthquake destroys much of San Francisco. Most of the damage comes from a fire caused by the quake that rages out of control for three days.

October 17, 1989: A magnitude-7.1 earthquake kills 68 people and causes $10 billion in damage. The quake becomes known as the World Series earthquake, because it disrupts Major League Baseball's World Series between the San Francisco Giants and the Oakland Athletics.

Commerce

From the times of earliest human settlement, commerce and industry along the Pacific coast have been based on the fruits of the land. Two of the earliest businesses that grew up along the coast were the fur and timber industries.

Fur and Timber

The first important industry along the Pacific coast was the trade in animal pelts. Two animals most prized for their skins were the sea otter and the seal. Fur hunting and trading were most common along the northern Pacific coast. In Alaska, the first permanent settlement was founded by Russian fur traders on Kodiak Island in 1784.

Oregon's first permanent settlement also began as a fur trading post. Fort Astoria was built in 1811 by John Jacob Astor, owner of the Pacific Fur Company. Located at the mouth of the Columbia River, Astoria was taken over by the British during the War of 1812 (1812–1815). The fur industry eventually died out in the 1840s after overhunting wiped out much of the beaver population.

Another important part of the early Pacific coast economy was the timber industry. Fir and pine were used to make the buildings of the West. The heavy forests of the coast, as well as those farther inland, proved so profitable that wood soon became known as "green gold." Coastal Washington was particularly well known for its large supply of timber.

One of the first timber companies along the Pacific coast was founded in San Francisco in 1849. Andrew Jackson Pope and Frederic Talbot traveled across the country from Maine to make their fortunes on the West Coast. At first, the two partners shipped lumber all the way from Maine. However, they soon realized that the northern Pacific coast was the perfect place for logging. They built the first steam sawmill in Washington, and business boomed.

In recent years, the timber industry has fallen on hard times. Laws to limit logging on federal land and to protect endangered animals in some forests have taken a toll. Competition from other nations that sell wood for less money has also hurt the U.S. timber industry. Today, fewer people than ever work in the timber industry along the northern Pacific coast.

Fishing

Fishing has played a major role in the lives of people living along the Pacific coast for thousands of years. The first fishers in the area were native people. Tribes on the northern coast carved out huge, wooden seagoing canoes. Armed with harpoons made of wood and mussel shells, they set out in search of whales and other sea creatures. In the south, tribes used nets to capture food from the sea.

Some Pacific coast towns got their starts as fishing villages. In Washington, for example, Oysterville was founded along the coast in 1854 by two oyster fishers. Oysters from the area were harvested, packaged, and shipped from the village to San Francisco.

Today, commercial (kuh-MER-shul) fishing is a huge industry off the Pacific coast. Each year, billions of dollars worth of seafood is taken from the Pacific waters by coastal fishing fleets. Sole, perch, flounder, cod, mackerel, and other fish are harvested from the Pacific. Shellfish is also an important part of the fishing industry, particularly in the northern Pacific waters. Shrimp and crab from Alaska are shipped around the world.

The fishing industry spawned many other businesses. Shipbuilders, for example, found the Pacific coast to be the perfect place to make wooden boats of all types. Not only were the coastal cities excellent (EK-sell-ent) locations for shipbuilding, but the nearby forests supplied the builders with all the timber that they needed for their ships. During the "golden age" of Pacific coast shipbuilding in the late nineteenth century (SEN-chur-ee), hundreds of ships were built in Pacific ports.

Another industry that got its start thanks to fishing was the fish processing industry. In early days, most fish processing took place in canneries. In the late 1800s, Alaska became a well-known center for canned

salmon. During the 1930s and 1940s, hundreds of sardine canneries dotted the Pacific coast from San Francisco to San Diego.

Inside the canneries, workers washed, cut, canned, and shipped the daily catch. Nothing went to waste. Even the sardine oil was used. Thousands of people worked in the sardine canneries. Many cannery workers were Chinese immigrants who had traveled to the Pacific coast in search of a better life. In Washington canneries, one out of every four workers was Chinese.

Commercial smelt fishermen pause for this photograph in Kelso, Washington, in 1910.

This 1852 daguerreotype (a nineteenth-century photograph) shows gold miners near Spanish Flat, California.

Mining

In the mid- and late 1800s, Americans caught gold fever. Beginning in 1849, thousands of miners and fortune hunters flooded to the foothills of the Sierra Nevada. The huge wave of people to the gold fields of California fueled the rapid development of many coastal cities. San Francisco especially (es-PESH-ul-ee) benefited from gold fever.

Thanks to the gold rush, San Francisco grew into an important shipping port. In seven months during 1849, nearly 700 ships sailed into San Francisco Bay. Most of them brought would-be millionaires from across the nation and around the world.

For those who were lucky enough to strike it rich, San Francisco was the city of dreams. A miner who had been lucky in the hills might come to San Francisco seeking companionship and excitement. Businesses to satisfy the new arrivals sprang up everywhere. Stores, banks, and hotels were erected to serve the miners—as were saloons, gambling parlors, and brothels.

ANTI-CHINESE DISCRIMINATION

One group of immigrants that began arriving during the California gold rush was the Chinese. Unfortunately, these new arrivals often faced discrimination, poverty, and hardship in the United States. Miners hoping to make their fortunes in the gold fields found that they had to pay a heavy tax to mine. Even Chinese business owners in San Francisco and other towns had to pay fees to run their businesses. During the 1870s and 1880s, Chinese neighborhoods were sometimes burned, and their residents were driven away. In 1882, a law was passed to keep Chinese immigrants out of the United States. The law was not repealed until 1943.

In 1880, Joe Juneau (JOO-noh) and Richard Harris discovered gold near what would one day become the city of Juneau, Alaska. Once word leaked out, miners turned their attention to the north. Juneau quickly became a boomtown. Because of the town's good port and good supply of lumber, some settlers remained in Juneau. Today, the city is Alaska's capital.

Oil was first discovered in Alaska in the early 1900s. However, the first large oil strike there was not made until 1957, on the Kenai (KEE-nye)

Peninsula. In 1968, it was discovered that the greatest wealth of oil deposits was located in northern Alaska, on the Arctic coast.

Oil companies needed to find an effective way of getting their oil from northern Alaska to the port cities on the Pacific coast. In 1974, work began on the Trans-Alaska Pipeline. The 800-mile (1,280-kilometer) pipeline stretches from Prudhoe Bay to the ice-free port city of Valdez. From Valdez, the oil is shipped down the Pacific coast to oil refineries in Washington and California.

Shipping

Shipping has always been an important industry along the Pacific coast. In the 1800s, ships to the coast brought settlers, gold miners, and immigrants from other countries. Ships left Pacific ports loaded with lumber, gold, fish, and other valuable natural resources from the region. Later, oil would become one of the most important products shipped along the coast.

Today, there are many busy ports up and down the Pacific coast. These ports include Anchorage (AN-kor-ihj), Alaska; Seattle (see-AT-ul), Washington; Portland, Oregon; and Los Angeles (los AN-jell-ess), Oakland, and San Francisco, California. Each year, billions of dollars worth of goods pass through these ports. These goods include cars, furniture, toys, petroleum, computers, and much more.

By volume of goods shipped, the Port of Los Angeles is the busiest port in the nation. It also has one of the world's largest artificial (ar-tih-FISH-ul) harbors. Eighty shipping lines operate out of the busy port, as do eight cruise lines. In 2001, nearly 2,900 vessels sailed in and out of the port. The port itself is located 20 miles (32 kilometers) south of Los Angeles, in San Pedro Bay. The first trading ship to sail into San Pedro Bay arrived in 1805. Construction of the Port of Los Angeles didn't begin until 1899.

The Trans-Alaska pipeline snakes its way across the Alaskan wilderness.

QUICK FACTS ABOUT THE TRANS-ALASKA PIPELINE

- The pipeline is 4 feet (1.2 meters) in diameter.

- More than half the length of the pipeline is above ground, while the rest is buried below ground.

- More than 2 million barrels of oil can be piped from Prudhoe Bay to the city of Valdez, Alaska, each day.

- The pipeline crosses three mountain ranges and more than 800 rivers and streams.

- Valdez received its 13 billionth barrel of oil through the pipeline on April 27, 2000.

The tanker Exxon Valdez was responsible for one of the worst oil spills in history.

THE *EXXON VALDEZ* DISASTER

In 1989, one of the worst environmental disasters in the history of the United States took place off the Pacific coast of Alaska. On March 23, the tanker *Exxon Valdez* set sail from Valdez on its way to deliver a cargo of oil to Long Beach, California. The ship ran aground in Prince William Sound in Alaska, spilling 11 million gallons (41.8 million liters) of oil into the ocean.

THE CITY OF ANGELS

In 1781, a group of forty-four Spanish settlers began building a small town that they named *El Pueblo de Nuestra Señora la Reina de los Ángeles de Porciúncula*, or "The Town of Our Lady the Queen of the Angels of Porciúncula." The town became known simply as Los Angeles. It grew slowly, and by 1800, only 315 people lived there. The town eventually became an important trading site, and by the 1840s, it was the largest town in Mexico's California territory. The United States took control of Los Angeles during the Mexican War (1846–1848). Immigration and the coming of the railroads fueled Los Angeles's population growth.

Today, Los Angeles is the second most populated city in the United States, behind New York City. With large Latino, black, and Asian populations, the city is a melting pot of cultures. An important—and glamorous—part of the city's economy is the entertainment industry. Hollywood, a section of L.A., is famous throughout the world as the center of the movie business.

Today

In recent years, the Pacific coast has seen an increase in its population. The coast's popularity also brings some problems with it. One serious problem is pollution. Air pollution, also called *smog*, is very bad, especially in California's urban areas.

California has taken several steps to control air pollution in regions around cities. Since the 1970s, state officials (uh-FISH-uls) have regulated auto emissions carefully. Cars that pollute too much must be fixed. California has also increased public transportation in an effort to cut down on the number of vehicles (VEE-ik-ulz) on the road. State officials look for ways to protect its waters and land areas from pollution, as well.

Tourism is a major part of the Pacific coast's economy. Sport fishing, swimming, surfing, and other water activities are common along the coastline. The beaches in southern California attract visitors year-round. Most of Oregon's coastline has been set aside for public use. Also each year, thousands travel to Alaska's Pacific coast to view the wild beauty of the many national parks and preserves there.

Rocky Mountains

5

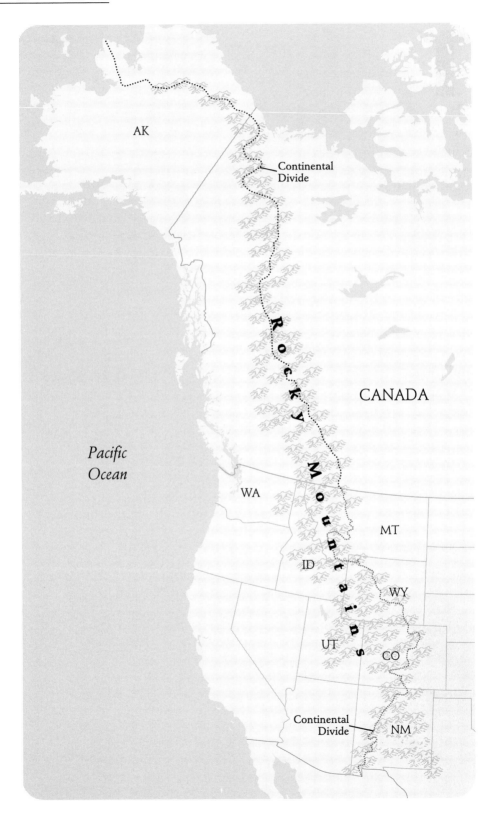

The Rocky Mountains are a major mountain system that stretches about 3,000 miles (4,800 kilometers) across the North American continent. The Rockies begin in Alaska and extend down through Canada and into the West, ending in central New Mexico in the Southwest region. Called the continent's backbone or spine, the Rockies are the largest mountain system in North America.

The Rockies run in a long, fairly straight line that is 350 miles (560 kilometers) wide in some areas. In the West, the Rockies cut through Alaska, Washington, Montana, Idaho, Wyoming, Utah, and Colorado. The Rockies are bordered by the Great Plains of the Midwest to the east and a series of basins and plateaus (plat-OHZ) to the west.

The Rockies are an area that is rich in minerals and other natural resources. With its high peaks, magnificent (mag-NIH-fih-sent) wildlife, and other majestic scenes, the region is also one of breathtaking beauty. As a result, the Rockies are home to many national parks and forests. The region is still lightly populated compared to many other parts of the nation, with fewer large cities than in other areas.

Majestic scenery has drawn visitors to Yellowstone National Park since it was established in 1872. Yellowstone was the first national park in the United States.

Settlement and Commerce

The Rocky Mountains are a relatively young mountain system. They began forming only about 100 million years ago. Over the centuries (SEN-chur-eez), the Rockies have been shaped by glaciers and worn away by wind and water. Even today, the mountains continue to grow and change.

The first people to live near the Rockies arrived about 10,000 years ago. These early people hunted the big mammals that moved through the area, including elk, bison, and bighorn sheep.

Before Europeans and Americans began exploring the Rockies, many tribes claimed territory near the mountains. These tribes included the Arapaho (uh-RAP-uh-hoh), Cheyenne (shye-ANN), Crow, Cree, and Shoshone (shoh-SHOH-nee). Other groups were the Apache (uh-PATCH-ee), Kiowa (KYE-oh-wa), Blackfoot, Salish (SAY-lish), and Nez Perce tribes. Most of the tribes lived near but not in the Rockies. They used the mountains as a hunting ground, as well as a sacred area.

> • *Fast Fact* •
>
> **Native Americans called the Rockies** *Mistakis*— **"backbone of the world."**

Exploring the Rockies

The first European to sight any part of the Rocky Mountains may have been Spanish conquistador (kohn-KEESS-tah-dor) Francisco Vásquez (fran-SISS-koh VAHS-kez) de Coronado. In 1540, Coronado ventured into the American Southwest searching (unsuccessfully) for the fabled Seven Cities of Gold. Coronado didn't explore the Rockies of the West. He saw only the Sangre de Cristo Mountains in New Mexico, of the Southwest region.

The first people to see the Rockies in the western United States were Pierre and Paul Mallet. In 1739, the two brothers caught their first glimpse of the Rockies' towering peaks as they explored the Arkansas (AR-ken-saw) River. However, these two early adventurers were not interested in exploring the Rockies further. They soon returned to New Orleans, Louisiana.

For years, the Rockies remained a huge obstacle, looming high over the Great Plains. After the United States acquired the mountains in the Louisiana Purchase, however, President Thomas Jefferson wanted to know more about the land. In 1805, he sent the first American expedition into the Rockies, led by Meriwether Lewis and William Clark. In 1805, the two adventurers, with the help of Native American guide Sacagawea (sak-uh-juh-WEE-uh), led a group over the Rockies in Montana. The group crossed the Continental Divide at the Lemhi (LEM-hye) Pass, traveling 300 miles (480 kilometers) on horseback through the mountains.

EXPLORING THE ROCKIES IN THE WESTERN UNITED STATES

Most of the early explorers of the Western Rockies were Americans who surveyed the area after the Louisiana Purchase.

Explorer	Country	Year	State Explored
Louis-Joseph and François Vérendrye	Canada	1743	Wyoming
Meriwether Lewis and William Clark	United States	1805	Montana
Zebulon Pike	United States	1806	Colorado
Robert Stuart	United States	1812	Wyoming
Stephen Long	United States	1820	Colorado
Benjamin Bonneville	United States	1832	Wyoming
John Wesley Powell	United States	1867	Colorado

During their journey, Lewis and Clark kept journals with detailed accounts of the people, wildlife, and vegetation that they saw along the way. These accounts of the Rockies and the land near the Pacific (puh-SIFF-ik) Ocean excited many people back east. Interest in exploring and settling the land to the west of the Rockies grew. The Lewis and Clark expedition marked the beginning of American settlement near and across the big mountains.

The second expedition sent by the American government into the Rockies was led by Zebulon Pike. A lieutenant (loo-TEN-ant) in the U.S. Army, Pike explored the Rockies in Colorado. Pike didn't have a high opinion of the Great Plains and Rocky Mountains. He compared the area to the deserts of Africa. Before long, the area was popularly known as the Great American Desert.

The last great exploratory journey into the Rockies was led in the early 1840s by John C. Frémont. Frémont, known today as "the Great Pathfinder," was guided through the mountains by Kit Carson and other mountain men. From 1841 to 1844, Frémont traveled the West, mapping much of the area beyond the Rockies. He also mapped the Oregon Trail, a path that would serve as one of the main routes for settlers into the Oregon Territory.

• Fast Fact •

In 1856, John C. Frémont was the first Republican candidate for president. Although Illinois (il-ih-NOY) lawyer Abraham Lincoln gave about fifty speeches in his support, Frémont was defeated by James Buchanan (byoo-KAN-an).

The Mountain Men

Even before Lewis and Clark ventured across the Great Divide, a small number of Europeans and Americans had been hunting and living in the mountains for years. These people had come to the

mountains to take advantage of the natural resources, *John C. Frémont* particularly the animals. These early fur trappers, *and his expedition* attracted by the plentiful supply of beavers in the *crossed the Rocky* *Mountains in* Rockies, became known as "mountain men." *1842.*

The first trappers began hunting in the Rockies in 1806, when John Colter left the Lewis and Clark expedition on the homeward journey. The following year, Colter met Manuel Lisa, founder of the Missouri Fur Company. Together, Colter and Lisa set up a trading post in the Rockies on the Yellowstone River.

At first, groups like the Missouri Fur Company, the Rocky Mountain Fur Company, and the American Fur Company traded with Native American tribes for the furs. However, companies soon began to send their own trappers into the wild. Eventually, many trappers struck out on their own. These "free trappers" braved hostile Native Americans, wild animals, and severe weather to earn themselves a living.

The life of the mountain man was hard and lonely. Dressed in animal skins, the trapper roamed the mountainsides, usually working alone. He carried his traps, along with a pistol, tomahawk, skinning knife, sharpening stone, and rifle. The mountain man spent the fall of each year trapping. In the winter, he settled down in the mountains to wait out the long, cold season. Then in the spring, he began trapping again.

Beaver trapping itself wasn't easy. The mountain man spent much of his time wading through icy cold water to set his beaver traps. Once the beaver was caught, the mountain man had to skin it and then scrape and dry the skin.

The highlight of the mountain man's year was the summer "rendezvous" (RAHN-day-voo). Each summer, the trappers would come out of the wilderness and meet with merchants who had traveled to the area from St. Louis. Also known as a "Rocky Mountain fair," the rendezvous gave trappers the chance to sell their furs or trade them for food and other supplies.

The event was also a social occasion for the trappers. Liquor, gambling, dancing, and games were all available. A lonely mountain man might even acquire a Native American wife to keep him company on the mountain. When the gathering ended, the trapper would head back into the mountains, and the cycle would begin again.

In the early 1800s, more than 600 mountain men trapped in the Rockies, near the Missouri River. By 1841, with the number of beaver and other animals getting smaller, the fur trade was dead. The last Rocky

RANGES OF THE ROCKIES

The Rockies themselves are made up of at least fifty separate mountain ranges. Some of the tallest peaks are found in the section known as the Southern Rockies, in Colorado and Wyoming. Rockies ranges include the following.

Range	States	Highest Mountain and Elevation
Absaroka Range	Montana, Wyoming	Frank's Peak, 13,140 feet (3,942 meters)
Bighorn Mountains	Montana, Wyoming	Cloud Peak, 13,166 feet (3,950 meters)
Brooks Range	Alaska	Mount Isto, 9,060 feet (2,718 meters)
Front Range	Colorado	Grays Peak, 14,270 feet (4,281 meters)
Gallatin Range	Montana, Wyoming	Electric Peak, 10,992 feet (3,298 meters)
San Juan Mountains	Colorado, *New Mexico	Uncompahgre Peak, 14,309 feet (4,293 meters)
Sangre de Cristo Mountains	Colorado, *New Mexico	Blanca Peak, 14,345 feet (4,304 meters)
Sawatch Range	Colorado	†Mount Elbert, 14,433 feet (4,333 meters)
Teton Range	Idaho, Wyoming	Grand Teton, 13,770 feet (4,131 meters)
Uinta Mountains	Utah, Wyoming	Kings Peak, 13,528 feet (4,123 meters)
Wind River Range	Wyoming	Gannett Peak, 13,804 feet (4,141 meters)

* Not a Western state   † Tallest peak in the Rockies

A herd of elk grazes below Mount Holmes in Yellowstone National Park.

• Fast Fact •

The *timberline* **of a mountain is the height above which trees cannot survive.**

Mountain fair was held in 1840. During their short time in the Rockies, the mountain men provided much-needed information about the area.

After the trade in beaver furs died away, the mountain men turned their attention in new directions. Many became guides, helping settlers and surveyors into, across, and out of the Rockies. The mountain men knew the peaks, rivers, and passes better than most. From 1840 to the 1860s, many made a good living leading pioneers to Oregon and California.

During this period, thousands passed over the Rockies to the land in the West. One of the most popular routes was the Oregon Trail. The Oregon Trail cut through the Rockies at South Pass, located in the Wind River Range in Wyoming. Former fur trading posts evolved into supply posts for the passing pioneers, including Bent's Fort in Colorado; Fort Laramie and Fort Bridger in Wyoming; and Fort Hall in Oregon.

MANIFEST DESTINY

As American settlers pushed farther westward, they were guided by the principle of Manifest Destiny, the belief that Americans were entitled to rule the entire North American continent from the Atlantic to the Pacific. The phrase was first used in 1845 by magazine editor John O'Sullivan. In his magazine, O'Sullivan claimed that the United States should take control of the Oregon Territory "by right of our manifest destiny to overspread and to possess the whole of the continent."

THE CONTINENTAL DIVIDE

The Continental Divide is a line in North America that separates rivers that flow east from those that flow west. In the United States, the Continental Divide generally (JEN-er-ul-lee) follows the crest of the Rocky Mountains. Rivers that rise in the Rockies and flow east toward the Atlantic Ocean include the Arkansas (AR-ken-saw), Missouri, and Yellowstone Rivers. Important rivers that flow west into the Pacific (puh-SIFF-ik) Ocean include the Columbia, Snake, Colorado, and Salmon Rivers. The first Americans to cross the "Great Divide" were Meriwether Lewis and William Clark in 1805.

Old Faithful is the most famous geyser in Yellowstone National Park. The geyser erupts, on average, every seventy-five minutes.

COLTER'S HELL

In 1807 and 1808, mountain man John Colter ventured into what is now Yellowstone National Park. He brought back tales of bubbling mud, hissing hot springs, and jets of water erupting from below the earth. Although most people who heard the stories of "Colter's Hell" thought that they were tall tales, one man believed them. William Clark included information he learned from Colter on a map of the West.

FAMOUS ROCKIES MOUNTAIN MEN

The mountain men, living in harsh conditions, quickly became legends in their own time.

Jim Bridger began his career as a mountain man at the age of seventeen. In 1824, he was the first American to see the Great Salt Lake. Bridger was the last of the mountain men, dying in 1881 at the age of seventy-seven.

The most famous of the mountain men, *Christopher "Kit" Carson* earned fame by guiding surveying and military expeditions through the Rockies. During the Civil War (1861–1865), Carson served in the Union army.

John Colter was captured by the Blackfoot tribe in 1808. He managed to escape by running away and hiding beneath a pile of logs in the middle of a river. Colter then walked more than 200 miles (320 kilometers) to safety.

This rock in Montana may have been inscribed by John Colter, a member of the Lewis and Clark expedition.

Jedediah Strong Smith was a famous mountain man who had a near-fatal run-in with a grizzly bear on his first expedition. His companions sewed his ear and part of his scalp back onto his head. Smith's luck ran out in 1831, when he was killed by members of the Comanche (kuh-MAN-chee) tribe in Kansas.

William Henry Ashley and *Andrew Henry*, owners of a Rocky Mountain fur company, organized the first mountain man rendezvous (RAHN-day-voo) in the summer of 1825.

Gold in the Hills

Gold was first discovered in the Rockies in 1858, west of what is now Denver, Colorado. Soon, thousands of potential millionaires were rushing to the Rockies. The cry "Pikes Peak or bust!" became a well-known slogan of the gold miners.

The gold rush marked the beginning of many new towns in the Colorado Rockies. The towns sprang up to serve the miners. In the saloons and gambling halls of the startup cities, a miner could forget his sorrows if he hadn't struck it rich. If he did find the precious gold metal, he could spend his hard-earned wealth in the same spots. Towns in Colorado that got their starts during the gold rush include Golden, Pueblo, and Boulder.

Another town to arise out of the Rockies gold rush was Denver. Founded as St. Charles Town in 1858, the town was purchased by William Larimer of Kansas. Larimer renamed his new town Denver. The town grew quickly. Even after the gold was gone, it continued to grow. Today, Denver is the largest city in Colorado, as well as the state's capital.

In the 1860s, gold was discovered in the Montana Rockies. As in Colorado, many towns grew out of the Montana rush. One such town was Helena, Montana's capital. Helena started out as Last Chance Gulch in 1864. The same year, Butte (BYOOT), another large Montana city, was founded. Butte's population really soared in 1874, after the discovery of copper there. The Anaconda Copper Company quickly bought up the area and began controlling the precious metal. By the turn of the next century, Butte Hill was known as the "richest hill on earth."

By the 1870s, gold was no longer the metal of choice in Colorado, either. At that time, the state became famous for its wealth of silver. One town that thrived on silver and lead was Leadville, Colorado. Although the town started as a gold-mining town, it boomed in the late 1870s with the discovery of lead and silver

This painting depicts Zebulon Montgomery Pike, the American army general and explorer for whom Pikes Peak in Colorado is named.

PIKES PEAK

Pikes Peak, more than 14,100 feet (4,230 meters) tall, is located in the Front Range of the Rocky Mountains. Discovered in 1806 by adventurer Zebulon Pike, the mountain was later named after the first American to lay eyes on it. Pike tried to climb to the top of the mountain but failed. After his unsuccessful attempt, Pike predicted that the mountain would never be scaled. He was proved wrong just fourteen years later by army engineer (en-jin-EER) Stephen Long. Today, a weather station stands on top of Pike's famous peak.

nearby. By 1880, 15,000 people lived in Leadville. Most of them worked in the silver-mining industry. Other "silver towns" included Aspen and Aurora.

The silver boom lasted for little more than two decades. By the early 1890s, the demand for the metal had decreased. That's when the U.S. government decided that silver would no longer be used as money.

While some towns managed to survive the gold and silver busts, others did not. One notable example of a town that died with the mines is Bannack, Montana. In the 1860s, Bannack was a thriving city that catered to gold miners. In 1864, the city was even chosen as the territorial capital of Montana. Today, Bannack is a ghost town. It has been protected by the National Park Service as a historic site since the 1950s. Visitors to Bannack can see Skinner's Saloon and Hotel Meade, remnants of a time long past.

Ghost towns such as this one can be found throughout the West. They are reminders of boom times in the past.

Today, mining is still an important part of the Rocky Mountain region's economy. Gold, lead, silver, copper, and other metals are still mined throughout the area. Mineral wealth in the form of coal and petroleum is also found there.

Other Commerce
in the Rockies

Miners weren't the only people who rushed into the Rocky Mountain area in the mid-1800s. In the 1860s, farmers began settling the area. They soon learned what the natives of the area had always known: The dry mountain soil was not good for growing crops. However, the mountainsides and valleys were perfect for grazing livestock.

Cattle ranchers were the first to stake out a living in the Rockies. Sheep farmers quickly followed. The cattlemen, however, did not want to share the grazing land and water supplies with the sheep farmers. Violent conflicts between the two groups soon arose.

From 1875 to the early 1900s, attacks on sheep farmers by cattle ranchers were common. In 1887, 2,600 sheep were burned in a corral near Laramie, Wyoming. That same year, 2,500 sheep were clubbed to death in Montana by night riders, and thousands more were driven over cliffs in Colorado. Some sheep farmers were also killed. In 1905, the forest service brought an end to the violence by administering permits to the ranchers.

The Transcontinental
Railroad

Before the 1860s, the Rockies were considered a remote location that few people would dare to visit. Only those willing to make the long, difficult, and dangerous trek from the East had ventured into the mountains. In 1867, however, everything changed when the Union Pacific Railroad reached the Rockies from the East.

The building of the railroad also led to the development of many towns along the way. Two Wyoming towns that flourished as workers' camps were Cheyenne and Laramie. These two towns later grew into important cities. Today, Cheyenne is Wyoming's capital, and Laramie is the third-largest town in the state.

Denver, Colorado, also received a boost from the new railroads. In 1870, the town built its own railway to connect it to Cheyenne and the other western rail lines. Denver quickly grew into an important trading town, with goods, services, and mining equipment coming and going.

> • Fast Fact •
>
> **Denver is known as "the Mile-High City" because it sits at an elevation of 1 mile (1.6 kilometers) above sea level.**

Tourism

opposite:
A skier rips down a challenging slope somewhere in the Rocky Mountains. Thousands of tourists visit the Rockies to ski each winter.

Tourism is an important part the of Rocky Mountain economy. Tourists began visiting the mountains in the 1880s. At that time, it was thought that the fresh air of the Rockies might cure tuberculosis and other ailments.

One of the most successful health resorts was in Colorado Springs, Colorado. The town boasted three healing springs: Iron, Soda, and Manitou (MAN-ih-too). The rich and famous flocked from the East, looking for fun, relaxation, and better health. By 1890, Colorado Springs was attracting 200,000 visitors a year.

Shortly before World War II (1939–1945), the mountains began attracting visitors of a different sort: skiers. In 1936, Swiss skier André Roch created the first ski trail on Aspen Mountain. Today, Aspen continues to be a popular ski resort. Other successful ski areas abound, including Vail and Steamboat Springs, Colorado, and Jackson Hole, Wyoming. Each year, millions of people travel to Colorado ski resorts.

opposite:
Buffalo still roam
the wilderness of
Yellowstone
National Park.

Today

Tourism continues to be very important in the Rockies today. In addition to skiing and other winter activities, national parks throughout the region draw millions of people each year. Popular destinations include Yellowstone, Glacier, and Rocky Mountain National Parks.

National parks have a long history in the Rocky Mountains. In the 1870s, people began to realize that timbering, mining, and other activities were damaging the land and wildlife. *Old-growth* forests had been cut down, destroying the habitats of many animals. Old-growth forests are forests that have been growing for many, many years. They have a well-developed ecosystem, with particular types of trees, plants, and wildlife. Destroying old-growth forests also destroys these ecosystems.

Some species (SPEE-sheez) of animals in the Rockies were hunted nearly to extinction by hunters and ranchers. (An *extinct* species has been completely wiped out.) These animals include grizzly bears, gray wolves, mountain lions, and bison (buffalo). In recent years, intense protection efforts and captive breeding programs have helped some former Rockies animals return to the wild. In *captive breeding programs*, endangered animals are bred in zoos or animal clinics. The young are later released into the wild.

CUTTING THROUGH THE ROCKIES

For more than a century, people had made their way from east to west across the Rocky Mountains. In 1968, construction began on a tunnel running through the Rockies. The Eisenhower Memorial Tunnel, completed in 1973, stretches more than 8,900 feet (2,670 meters) underneath the Continental Divide in Colorado. It is one of the longest land tunnels in the United States. Located 11,000 feet (3,300 meters) above sea level, it is also the highest land tunnel in the world. Each day, more than 26,000 cars travel through it.

YELLOWSTONE NATIONAL PARK

LAKE VILLAGE   1
WEST THUMB   21

CANYON VILLAGE 16
OLD FAITHFU

- Yellowstone National Park is located in the Gallatin, Washburn, and Absaroka Ranges in northwestern Wyoming, Montana, and Idaho.

- Established in 1872, Yellowstone was the world's first national park.

- The park covers more than 2.2 million acres (880,000 hectares).

- Yellowstone is known for its many geysers, hot springs, mud volcanoes, and *fumaroles*, which are holes in the ground that emit steam and gas.

- The most famous of Yellowstone's geysers is Old Faithful, which erupts about every seventy-five minutes. Other geysers include Steamboat, Sapphire (SAF-fye-er), Porkchop, and Minute Man Geysers.

Today, national parks in the Rockies are facing new types of problems. Over the years, a huge increase in the number of visitors to the parks has put a strain on many of them. Other stresses include acid rain and other types of pollution. To address pollution problems, the Environmental Protection Agency (EPA) recently passed rules to control pollution from factories near some national parks.

GRAND TETON NATIONAL PARK

The Grand Teton Mountains are known for jagged peaks and rugged terrain.

- Grand Teton National Park is located in the Teton Range in northwestern Wyoming.

- The park was established in 1929 and covers more than 309,000 acres (123,600 hectares).

- The Tetons are the youngest range in the Rockies, formed only about 9 million years ago.

- The park includes part of the Snake River, as well as Jackson Hole, a long narrow valley that is popular with skiers.

GLACIER NATIONAL PARK

Glacier National Park provides over 1 million acres (400,000 hectares) of protected habitat for native plants and animals of the Rocky Mountain region.

- Glacier National Park is located in the Lewis Range in northwestern Montana.

- The park was established in 1910 and covers more than 1 million acres (400,000 hectares).

- Glacier National Park is the only national park that is shared with Canada. In Canada, the park is called Waterton Lakes National Park. Together, the parks are called Waterton-Glacier International Peace Park. This international park was established in 1932 by both countries as "a symbol of permanent peace and friendship."

- The park takes its name from the large glaciers found there. There are about fifty moving glaciers in the park.

ROCKY MOUNTAIN NATIONAL PARK

Rocky Mountain National Park spans the Continental Divide.

- Rocky Mountain National Park is located in the Front Range in northern Colorado.

- The park was established in 1915 and covers more than 265,000 acres (106,000 hectares).

- Rocky Mountain National Park includes more than 100 peaks that are above 10,000 feet (3,000 meters).

- There are about 155 lakes within the park.

Sierra
Nevada

6

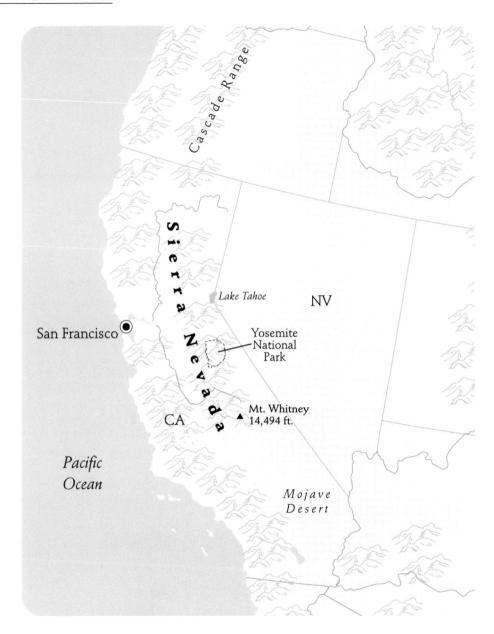

The Sierra Nevada is a mountain range that stretches about 400 miles (640 kilometers) through California and into Nevada. The range extends from the Cascade Range to the Mojave (moh-HAHV-ee) Desert. The Sierra is the longest unbroken range of mountains in the continental United States. In all, the range covers about 15.5 million acres (6.2 million hectares) of land.

The highest peaks in the range are in the section known as the High Sierra. The High Sierra is located to the south. Peaks here range from 6,000 feet (1,800 meters) to more than 14,000 feet (4,200 meters) in height. The highest peak in the range is Mount Whitney in California, which measures 14,494 feet (4,348 meters) in height. Mount Whitney is the highest peak in the continental United States.

A climber makes her way up Mount Whitney, the highest peak in the continental United States.

A number of important rivers flow through the Sierra Nevada, including the San Joaquin (hoh-ah-KEEN), Tuolumne (too-AHL-eh-mee), American, Feather, and Merced. Lake Tahoe in the Sierras is North America's third-deepest lake. The lake, which measures 22 miles (35 kilometers) by 12 miles (19 miles) in size, has a maximum depth of 1,645 feet (4,941 meters).

TALL SIERRA PEAKS

The Sierra Nevada is home to a number of peaks that tower over 14,000 feet (4,200 meters) above sea level. In general, the eastern side of the Sierra has higher peaks. The western side has been more severely eroded over time by wind and rain. Here are a few of the highest peaks in the Sierra.

Mountain	Elevation
Mount Whitney	14,494 feet (4,348 meters)
Mount Williamson	14,375 feet (4,313 meters)
North Palisade	14,242 feet (4,273 meters)
Keeler Needle	14,239 feet (4,272 meters)
Mount Sill	14,153 feet (4,246 meters)
Mount Russell	14,088 feet (4,226 meters)
Polemonium Peak	14,080 feet (4,224 meters)
Split Mountain	14,042 feet (4,213 meters)

Settlement

The earliest humans to live in the Sierra Nevada arrived there thousands of years ago. These early tribes of Native Americans lived in the foothills on both sides of the range. Tribes often crossed through mountain passes in order to trade with one another.

Tribes of the Sierra included the Miwok (MEE-wok), Maidu (MYE-doo), Washo, Mono, and Paiute

(PYE-yoot). They were in the Sierra long before Europeans and Americans began exploring the region. The tribes hunted deer and other small game and foraged for nuts, acorns, and berries.

The first crossing of the Sierra Nevada by an American took place in 1827, when Jedediah Strong Smith crossed the range on his way east from California. Smith, a fur trader and explorer, had been ordered out of California by the Spanish governor of the region. The Spanish did not want Americans exploring their territory.

More than fifteen years later, another adventurer braved the Sierra range. In 1843, famed explorer John C. Frémont, guided by Kit Carson, crossed the Sierra Nevada in the dead of winter. Frémont's descriptions of his travels popularized the West as a destination for pioneers and settlers.

JOHN C. FRÉMONT—SOLDIER, EXPLORER, POLITICIAN

John Frémont got his first taste of adventuring as a young man in the army. In 1839, he joined French explorer Joseph Nicolas Nicollet on a trip to map the region between the Mississippi and Missouri Rivers. Frémont began his own adventuring three years later, when he was commissioned to lead the first of three trips into the Oregon Territory. Frémont and Kit Carson explored and mapped the Oregon Trail, the Columbia River, the Sierra Nevada, and the Great Basin. Frémont played a key role in California's fight for independence (in-duh-PEN-dense) from Mexico. He later served California as governor and as U.S. senator. Fremont Peak in the Wind River Mountains is named for him, as is Fremont, California.

In the 1840s, the first settlers began crossing the Sierra Nevada. Most crossed through the passes first used by Native American tribes in the region. These paths would soon take on American names. Famous, well-traveled passes through the Sierra included the Donner, Ebbets, Beckwourth, and Carson Passes. Many years later, these passes would be covered by railroad tracks or paved over for highways.

One of the most infamous passes was the Donner Pass, located north of Lake Tahoe. The pass was named for the Donner Party, a group of eighty-seven settlers that set out for the West in 1846. They began their journey in Springfield, Illinois (il-ih-NOY). In Nevada, the party's leader made the fateful decision to take a shortcut that was not well mapped.

The new route, called the Hastings Cutoff, led the group through the Great Salt Lake Desert, a long and perilous stretch of land. The "shortcut" delayed them, and when they finally arrived at the Sierra Nevada, they were short of food and exhausted from their nightmarish trek through the desert.

An early winter snowstorm sealed the fate of many of the party members. Forced to seek shelter in the Sierras, they could do nothing but wait out the winter and hope for rescue. During the winter, many of the party starved to death. The others were forced to eat the dead bodies in order to survive. When rescuers finally arrived in March 1847, only forty-seven of the original (oh-RIJ-ih-nal) eighty-seven were still alive.

In the twentieth century (SEN-chur-ee), the Sierra Nevada was the site of Manzanar, an *internment camp* where people of Japanese descent were held as prisoners during World War II (1939–1945). During this war, Japan was one of the countries against which the United States was fighting. In February 1942, President Franklin D. Roosevelt signed an act that ordered thousands of Japanese to be taken from their homes and placed in the camps. More than 120,000 Japanese people were confined during the war. Most of these people were U.S. citizens.

• Fast Fact •

In 1988, President Ronald Reagan issued an official apology (uh-PAHL-uh-jee) to Japanese-Americans interned during World War II (1939–1945).

Manzanar was the first of ten internment camps to be opened in the West. Located in Owens Valley, the camp was on the site of an old apple orchard. It was run like

a prison, complete with barbed wire and armed guards who patrolled the grounds to prevent escape. Detainees lived in tiny rooms. They faced sweltering heat during the summer, freezing cold during the winter, and frequent dust storms. Manzanar was finally closed in November 1945.

This photograph shows the Manzanar internment camp as it was during World War II. In 1997, the camp was reopened for tours after being closed for more than forty years.

Commerce

Until 1848, most Americans looked at the Sierra Nevada range as an obstacle to be passed over as quickly and painlessly as possible. That year, however, a man named James Marshall discovered the first hint of the amazing mineral wealth in the mountains. Before long, the rush to the Sierra Nevada would set off one of the largest mass migrations to the West ever seen. This mass migration would forever change California and the West.

Gold in the Hills

A faithful replica of Sutter's Mill that looks very much like the original depicted in this painting is located near the original site in Coloma, California.

On January 24, 1848, a worker named James Marshall was building a sawmill on the South Fork of the American River. Marshall noticed some shiny flakes in the water. He collected the flakes and showed them to the mill's owner, John Sutter. The two realized that Marshall had discovered gold. They agreed to keep the find quiet.

The secret soon leaked out, however. Those who heard the news rushed to Sutter's Mill, located in a small valley on the western slope of the Sierra Nevada. Before long, even President James K. Polk had heard about the gold. To encourage settlement in the territory of California, Polk announced to Congress that the gold fields of California might be the site of untold riches. People from all over the nation immediately packed up and headed to the Sierras. The gold rush was on!

During the height of the gold rush, thousands of miners poured into the Sierra foothills. Captains and crews deserted their ships in the harbor in San Francisco (san fran-SISS-koh), leaving them to rot in the bay. Bankers, lawyers, schoolteachers, and others left their families behind for months, hoping to return rich. These would-be millionaires became known as "forty-niners," named for the year in which gold fever hit the hardest. By 1850, more than 250,000 people had come to California.

FAMOUS FORTY-NINERS

This 1851 painting shows John Sutter, the owner of the mill where gold was first discovered in California.

John Sutter was the man whose mill started it all. Sutter didn't get rich off his gold. Instead, he was swindled out of his lands and his home was burned down. Sutter died in poverty.

Gold fever attracted miners from all around the world. The gold rush was responsible for the migration of thousands of Chinese. Others traveled from Europe, South and Central America, and Australia. Some struck it rich. Others returned home poor and disheartened. Many of the recent immigrants decided to stay and make a new life in the United States.

FAMOUS FORTY-NINERS

Lotta Crabtree began her career singing and dancing for gold miners during the California gold rush. She later became a world-famous actress.

Lotta Crabtree was a world-famous singer and dancer who got her start in the gold mines of the Sierra Nevada at the age of six. Crabtree charmed homesick miners by dancing Irish jigs and reels and singing tearful ballads. She later gained worldwide acclaim as an actress.

Life as a Miner

At first, gold was so plentiful that the early miners could pick it from the streams. *Panning* did the trick. Panning for gold was a monotonous chore. Miners spent the day crouched over streams, sometimes standing in icy water. They scooped water and soil from the streambed into shallow pans, which they swirled so that the lighter materials, such as sand and soil, washed out. Gold, much heavier than water or sand, settled to the bottom of the pan. Miners worked from dawn until dusk at this tedious chore.

As more people arrived, the river and stream banks became crowded. Soon, miners were lined up on the sides of the creeks, working side by side. Later arrivals learned that finding the gold was not as easy as they had been led to believe. Gold was not paving the bottom of every creek and river in the area.

While searching for their fortunes, miners lived in tents in mining camps. The camps were often given colorful names, reflecting the miners' hopes and sense of humor. Camp names included Rich Bar, Bedbug, You Bet, Poverty Flat, and Whiskeytown.

Life in the camps was rough. Dishonest merchants made their own riches by selling food and supplies at very high prices. However, a few things were cheap and easy to find in the camps: gambling, alcohol, prostitution, and trouble.

When miners were successful, their camps prospered and grew. Some of the camps developed into towns and then into cities. Placerville (PLASS-er-vill), California, for example, got its start as a mining town. The town was originally (oh-RIJ-ih-nal-ee) known as Hangtown, because the residents were quick to string up criminals.

One of the most successful towns that developed during the gold rush was Sacramento, California. The area that became Sacramento was originally owned by John Sutter, who called it New Helvetia. When gold was discovered a few miles away, the town became an important supply center for gold miners. In 1854, it was named California's capital.

San Francisco, although not in the Sierras, also benefited from the gold rush. When gold was first discovered, San Francisco's population was just 800. During the gold rush, the town's harbor became the entry point for people sailing from other parts of the United States, as well as from around the world. The town quickly grew into a thriving center of trade, banking, shipping, and transportation.

FAMOUS FORTY-NINERS

Levi Strauss built a clothing factory in San Francisco, California, to manufacture tough denim clothing for the miners of the gold rush.

Levi Strauss was a Jewish immigrant from Bavaria. Strauss arrived in San Francisco (san fran-SISS-koh) in 1853. Learning that miners needed strong, durable pants, he designed a pair out of canvas. Before long, he switched from canvas to denim, dyed deep blue. Levi's jeans are still made today.

Although mining in the Sierras would continue for more than a century, the gold rush itself lasted only until 1858. By this time, the gold was no longer easy to find. Many miners moved on to other mineral-rich areas, including the Comstock Lode in Nevada's Great Basin.

Some miners stayed in the area, digging deep into the mountains for the precious ore. Others tried the *hydraulic* method of mining. They used giant hoses that shot out high-powered streams of water to blast away the mountainsides and riverbanks. Hydraulic mining ruined much of the mountain ecosystem.

From 1848 to 1948, more than $2 billion in gold was taken from the Sierra Nevada. Most of the gold taken from the Sierras came from the west side. On the east side, only small amounts of gold were found. One area on the eastern slopes where gold was found was Bodie. At its height, from 1859 to 1890, the town of Bodie had 10,000 residents and sixty-five saloons. It became known for its violence and lawlessness. Today, the town is a ghost town that is maintained as a state historic park.

• Fast Fact •

The phrase "bad man from Bodie" was coined in the 1880s to describe a person who was violent and lawless.

Two other industries that have been important in the Sierra Nevada are logging and ranching. Logging got its start as a result of the mining industry. The wooded areas around Lake Tahoe, for example, were cleared of pine during the early days of the gold rush. The wood was used to shore up mines being dug into the mountains.

After mining died down, logging became the region's top industry. Over the years, thousands of acres were stripped of timber on the Sierra slopes. Some of this timber was used to build the Central Pacific (puh-SIFF-ik) railroad tracks. In 1869, the Central Pacific joined up with the Union Pacific Railroad in Utah to form the nation's first transcontinental railroad.

Timber from the Sierras was also used to build homes and other buildings throughout California. As more and more people settled in the state, the demand for wood for buildings rose. Some historians believe that by the end of the 1800s, about one-third of the Sierra Nevada's forests had been cleared to supply the building booms in the West.

Ranching is another important part of the Sierra economy. Some unlucky miners decided to stay in the region and turned to farming and livestock instead of mining. Today, cattle ranching continues in the foothills of the Sierras.

The view of Yosemite Valley, with Half Dome in the background, has not changed since John Muir first visited the area more than 100 years ago.

JOHN MUIR AND THE SIERRA CLUB

John Muir (MYOOR) was a Scottish immigrant who fell in love with the wild beauty of the West. Muir first visited the Sierra Nevada in 1868. He spent the next six years studying the range's glaciers, as well as Yosemite (yoh-SEM-it-ee) valley. In 1889, Muir worked hard to get federal protection for the area. The following year, Congress established Yosemite and Sequoia (seh-KOY-uh) National Parks. In 1892, Muir helped found the Sierra Club. The group's mission was to protect America's wild places. Today, the Sierra Club has more than 700,000 members around the nation.

Tourism

Every year, people from around the world are attracted to the Sierra Nevada by the breathtaking views and wealth of activities. Visitors to the region can boat, raft, hike, ski, and climb the many steep mountain ranges. The area is also home to several national parks. Yosemite (yoh-SEM-it-ee), one of the oldest national parks in the United States, was founded in the Sierra Nevada in 1890.

One popular tourist destination in the region is Lake Tahoe. Lake Tahoe became a favorite destination after World War II. Today, the Lake Tahoe region has fifteen major ski resorts. Gambling, legal here, attracts many visitors. Nearby Squaw Valley was host to the 1960 Winter Olympics and is home to a U.S. Olympic training center.

AMAZING SIERRA SIGHTS

- One of the most famous Sierra sights, *El Capitan*, is a 3,593-foot (1,078-meter) granite *monolith*, a single block of stone that towers over Yosemite Valley.

- *Half Dome* is a 4,733-foot (1,420-meter) granite peak that got its name because half of it was sheared off by glaciers.

- *Yosemite Falls* are made up of three different levels. Together, the upper, lower, and middle falls drop more than 2,425 feet (728 meters), making Yosemite Falls the tallest in the United States.

- The *General Sherman Tree* is a huge sequoia that has been growing for more than 2,300 years. It measures 275 feet (83 meters) in height and 102 feet (31 meters) around its base. Other big, old sequoias in Sequoia National Park include the President, Chief Sequoyah, and General Lee.

- *Kings Canyon* is a national park that was founded in 1890. The park contains the highest canyon wall—more than 8,350 feet (2,505 meters) in height—in the United States.

Today

The national parks in the Sierra Nevada are some of the most popular in the nation. Yosemite is so popular that in recent years, the park service has worried about overcrowding and pollution from too many cars. As a result, the park service has asked visitors to leave their cars in parking lots and take buses into the park.

Lake Tahoe is another area that is fighting to retain its natural character. New development has led to pollution of the lake, as well as overcrowding. The development has also destroyed some marshland areas.

In recent years, several groups have formed to slow development in the Sierra. These groups hope to ensure that the mountain range retains its natural beauty for generations (jen-er-AY-shunz) to come.

Sources

BOOKS

Behrens, June. *Missions of the Central Coast.* Minneapolis: Lerner Publications, 1996.

Dannenberg, Julie. *Amidst the Gold Dust: Women Who Forged the West.* Golden, Colorado: Fulcrum Publishing, 2001.

Doherty, Kieran. *Explorers, Missionaries, and Trappers.* Minneapolis: Oliver Press, 2000.

Glass, Andrew. *Mountain Men: True Grit and Tall Tales.* New York: Doubleday Books for Young Readers, 2001.

Lawlor, Laurie. *Window on the West: The Frontier Photography of William Henry Jackson.* New York: Holiday House, 1999.

Pendergast, Tom and Sara. *Westward Expansion: Primary Sources.* Detroit: U.X.L., 2001.

Sherrow, Victoria. *Life During the Gold Rush.* San Diego: Lucent Books, 1998.

Uschan, Michael. *Westward Expansion.* San Diego: Lucent Books, 2000.

WEB SITES

The American West *www.americanwest.com*

DesertUSA *www.desertusa.com*

eHawaiiGov *www.hawaii.gov*

Exxon Valdez Oil Spill Trustee Council—Home Page *www.oilspill.state.ak.us/index.html*

Great Basin Web *www.greatbasinweb.com*

The Mountain Men: Pathfinders of the West 1810–1860 *xroads.virginia.edu/~HYPER/HNS/Mtmen/home.html*

University of North Dakota—Volcano World *volcano.und.edu/*

Utah State Historical Society—Utah History to Go *www.utahhistorytogo.org*

Index